Eros Celebrated

A Candid Translation and Commentary on the Erotic Love Poetry of Solomon's Song of Songs

Randal Cutter

Eros Celebrated

Copyright © 2026 Randal Cutter

All rights reserved worldwide.

ISBN-13: 979-8-9953304-0-0

New Testament Scripture quotations taken from the New Charismatic Bible, the New Testament Copyright © 2024 by Randal Cutter. Used with permission. All rights reserved worldwide.

The translation of the Song of Songs is a part of the New Charismatic Bible, the Old Testament (prepublication). Copyright © 2025 by Randal Cutter. Used with permission. All rights reserved worldwide.

The "New Charismatic Bible" text may be quoted in any form (written, visual, electronic, or audio), up to and inclusive of two hundred (200) verses without the express written permission of the publisher, providing the verses quoted do not amount to a complete book of the Bible nor do the verses quoted account for twenty-five percent (25%) or more of the total text of the work in which they are quoted. For such uses, notice of copyright must appear on the title or copyright page as listed above.

When quotations from the New Charismatic Bible text are used by a local church in non-saleable media such as church bulletins, orders of service, posters, overhead transparencies, or similar materials, a complete copyright notice is not required; however, the title, "New Charismatic Bible," or its abbreviation, "TNCB," must appear at the end of each quotation.

Permission requests that exceed the above General Use Guidelines must be directed to and approved in writing by New Dawn Publishing, 9955 NW 31st Street, Coral Springs, FL 33065, USA.

Distributed by: New Dawn Publishing
9955 NW 31st Street
Coral Springs, FL 33065
www.newdawn.org

DEDICATION

To the One who helped me understand what
He has hidden in His Word;

With special thanks to Bobby Conner,
Who heard the Word of the Lord
And gave this assignment.

With deep love for my wife, Dawn,
Who has been my marriage partner,
And has helped me appreciate
The contents of this Greatest Song
Through our love for each other.

Table of Contents

PREFACE

In early June of 2023, a prophetic friend visited our congregation. Bobby Conner stood before us on a Sunday morning, and, in the middle of his message, turned to me and said something that would change the trajectory of our Sunday mornings for months to come: "You need to do a series on the Song of Solomon. Answer the question, 'Who is this coming out of the wilderness leaning on her beloved?'" Then he explained that the Church is about to have a whole makeover all across America, and we need to identify who's coming up out of the wilderness with her beloved.

While I took what Bobby said very seriously, I wasn't excited. The Song of Songs has puzzled believers for millennia. I had always heard that the ancient rabbis wouldn't let anyone under thirty years old read it. One contemporary rabbi told me that the reader should also be married, even if he is thirty. He understood the power of the imagery in the book.

Over the millennia, commentators have allegorized the Song to the point of parody, pressing every detail to mean something spiritual—often with interpretations that say more about the interpreter's imagination than about the Song's intent. Others have avoided it altogether, uncomfortable with its earthy language and explicit celebration of married love.

But as Bobby spoke that Sunday morning, I knew this wasn't just his idea. Three weeks earlier, I'd had a dream with him in it. In that dream, he had walked up to me and said, "You've been saying Greek is fire to you, but now Hebrew is fire to you!"

When I woke up from the dream, I realized I'd never actually said those words about the Greek of the New Testament, but since I had translated most of the New Testament by the time of the dream (and since then, I have published it), I can say that I had been feeling very comfortable and confident in my Greek translation work. So, the message of the dream was clear to me: it was time to turn to Hebrew, to the Hebrew Scriptures, what Christians call the Old Testament. I knew I was supposed to continue the translation work to which the Lord had called me, but now in the Old Testament. The clear promise of the dream was that I would soon feel the same way about my work in Hebrew translation as I did with the Greek translation.

As a result, when Bobby showed up in person and gave me this specific assignment, I knew I was to begin my Hebrew translation in earnest, starting with the Song of Songs.

This commentary on the Song of Songs is the fruit of that Sunday morning.

INTRODUCTION

The Title of this Book

I have entitled this book Eros Celebrated because the Song of Songs certainly portrays sexual love (Eros) as something that is sacred, pure, and to be exuberantly enjoyed within the context of marriage. Solomon's Song clearly celebrates sexual love and desire. It declares that it is something holy and pure, and to be lauded.

Marriage is most certainly intended by our God to be erotic, in the best sense of the word. The Song of Songs presents the reader with the certain knowledge that, at least within a believing context, sexual love (Eros) enjoys God's full approval.

The title Eros Celebrated captures this perfectly. The late John White wrote Eros Defiled over fifty years ago, and later Eros Redeemed—both worthy contributions. But the Song of Songs goes beyond defilement and redemption. It celebrates. It celebrates God's relationship with his people, and the physical relationship of a husband and wife, which pictures that relational love. That celebration will echo for all eternity.

The Song by Any Other Name

The book we're studying is called "The Song of Songs" in Hebrew—Shir HaShirim. This is the Hebrew way of expressing the superlative. You could also call this book "The Greatest Song" or "The Best Song." The structure in Hebrew—two words together like this—creates the superlative, just as "Holy of Holies" means the Most Holy Place, and "King of Kings" means the greatest King. But in Christian circles, it is far more common to simply call it "The Song of Songs," or even "The Song of Solomon," since Solomon wrote it.

Four Layers of Interpretation

As we journey through this book together, we need to understand that there are at least four interpretive layers, four ways this book speaks to those who read it.

First, it is about Solomon and his bride. This is the most obvious layer. It is a series of love poems between King Solomon and a young woman identified as the Shulammite. It's earthy. It's explicit. It's a celebration of married love between a man and a woman. This layer is undeniable and essential. God put this in his Word to show us that he created and blessed sexual love between husband and wife.

Second, it reflects God's relationship with his people. When this was written, that meant God and Israel. Throughout the Hebrew prophetic scriptures, we see that God married Israel. Thus, she is called an adulteress when she turns away from God. You can only commit adultery against someone if you're married to that person. God views his covenant with Israel as a marriage relationship. This book celebrates that divine romance using human imagery.

Third, and growing out of that same covenant story, this book, for Christians, is ultimately a commentary on Christ and his spiritual bride, the Church. From a Christian perspective (See Ephesians 5:25-32), what began with God and Israel finds its fullest expression here. Every picture of Solomon pursuing his bride, every expression of love, every test and triumph—it's all a picture of Jesus and his Church. We are the bride he died for, the one he is preparing and maturing.

Fourth, it can also serve as a practical guide for married couples. Throughout this book, we see Solomon and the Shulammite working to keep their relationship "fresh and green." They complement each other, they create atmosphere, they pursue one another. While this isn't the primary purpose of the book, it is an undeniable gift woven through its pages: Godly marriages should reflect the passion and commitment we see here. Where the text offers practical wisdom for husbands and wives, I will point it out along the way.

The Key That Unlocks Everything

As I worked through translating this book from Hebrew, I knew there was something here, something profound, but I couldn't quite grasp the central message. Then, one night, I had a dream. All night long—and it was all night long—the Lord kept bringing me back to one Scripture reference, one verse. It came back over and over and over. It repeated so many times that when I woke up the next morning, I knew I had to study that particular verse in depth.

That verse is Song of Songs 8:10. It gave me the key to understanding the entire book, and it will be waiting for us in the final chapter of the book.

My hope is that as you walk through this practical commentary, the Song of Songs will come alive for you—not as an ancient curiosity or an embarrassing book to skip over, but as a living celebration of the love God has for you, and the intimacy he invites you to enjoy.

A Note on Translation

The translation you'll be reading in this commentary is my own, translated directly from the Hebrew. I've been translating the New Testament for years and published a complete New Testament translation in 2025. I approach Scripture with deep respect and care. When I translate, I'm not trying to smooth everything out or make it fit our cultural sensibilities. I'm trying to hear what the original text said in its original context.

The Song of Songs is earthy. It's explicit. The rabbis didn't let young people read it for good reason—not because it's dirty, but because it's honest about the beauty and power of married love. That honesty presents a challenge for the translator: how do you faithfully render what God inspired without being vulgar on one hand, or on the other hand, sanitize it so thoroughly that the meaning is lost?

My solution has been to produce two versions. The first I call The Veiled Version—a more tactful translation suited for public reading, which will appear in a future edition of my translation of the complete Hebrew Bible. The second version, and the one you hold in your hands, I call The Unveiled Version. Here, I have not attempted to soften the Song's language. I have, however, translated in a way that honors the beauty of the original without descending into vulgarity. I trust the mature reader will appreciate the expressions of love between Solomon and his bride for what they are—sacred and beautiful.

One more thing the reader should know: some of the Song's imagery won't make immediate sense to modern ears. When Solomon tells his bride her hair is like goats leaping down Mount Gilead, we are puzzled. When he praises her for having all her teeth, we're not particularly impressed—we expect a full set of teeth in our culture. But in their world, these were profound compliments. Throughout this commentary, I'll do my best to help you understand the cultural context behind the imagery, but I won't force modern equivalents into the text.

The Word of God stands as it is, and it's powerful enough to speak across cultures and centuries.

What to Expect

This journey will take us through valleys and mountaintops. We will see the first bloom of love, full of passion and excitement. We will encounter tests—the test of absence, the test of inconvenience. We will watch as the bride makes a costly mistake and faces consequences. We will see her restored, humbled, and growing in ways that only real failure can produce. We will arrive, finally, at that stunning moment when the mature bride emerges from the wilderness, leaning completely on her Beloved, reflecting his character so fully that people identify her by a form of his name.

Along the way, we will learn about spiritual warfare, about keeping our relationship with Jesus fresh, about God's jealous love for us, and about what it means to create an atmosphere for intimacy with God and press through when he feels distant.

We will also discover that this ancient love poem, written three thousand years ago, is actually about us—about God's people, even in the twenty-first century. This book is not a "How to" guide on becoming the mature bride. But it does point the way. And it is about believers throughout the ages, including you and me, who are learning to become the bride our God deserves.

1
THE FIRST BLOOM OF LOVE

Song of Songs Chapter One

1Solomon's Song of Songs:

The Shulammite

2"Let him kiss me with the kisses from his mouth—for your
lovemaking[1] is sweeter than wine. 3Your lotions have an
aromatic fragrance; your name is oil poured from one vessel
to another; therefore, the young women love you. 4Carry me
off after you; let us run!

"The king brought me to his bedroom."

The Daughters of Jerusalem

"Let us shout in exultation and delight in you; let us praise your lovemaking more than wine."

The Shulammite

"Rightly they love you.

5"I am dark but lovely, daughters of Jerusalem, like the tents of
Kedar, like the tent curtains of Solomon. 6Do not look at

[1] "Lovemaking" could also be translated "intimate love," "sexual intercourse," or "sexual intimacies." (See the use of this word in Ezekiel 16:8 where the young woman is described as old enough for sexual intimacy.)

me, for the sun has tanned me, and my complexion is dark.
The sons of my mother have been angry with me. They
made me tend the vineyards, but my own vineyard I have
not tended.

7“Tell me, you who my soul loves, where do you graze your
flocks? Where do you give them rest at noon? For why
should I be like one who veils herself by the flocks of your
companions?”

Solomon

8“If you do not know by yourself, O loveliest of women, go out
following the hoof-prints of the flock and graze your young
goats by the tents of the shepherds.

9“My intimate companion, I liken you to a mare for the
chariots of Pharaoh. 10Your cheeks are beautiful with
jewelry, your neck with strings of pearls.

11We will make jewelry of gold for you, studded with silver.”

The Shulammite

12“When the king was on his couch, my perfumed lotion
released its fragrance. 13My lover is a sachet of myrrh to me,
spending the night between my breasts. 14My lover is a
cluster of henna in the vineyards of Engedi.”

Solomon

15“Look how beautiful you are, my intimate companion; how
beautiful you are; your eyes are doves.”

The Shulammite

16“Look how handsome you are, my lover, and so pleasant.
Truly our bed is fresh and green. 17The timber-work of our
house is cedar; our rafters are juniper.”

Song of Songs Chapter Two (Verses 1-7)

The Shulammite

1“I am the rose of Sharon, a lily of the valleys.”

Solomon

2“As a lily between the thorns, so my intimate companion is among the daughters of Jerusalem.”

The Shulammite

3“As an apricot among the trees of the woodland, so my lover is
among the sons of Jerusalem. I delighted greatly and rested
in his shade, and his fruit was sweet to my taste. 4He
brought me to the vineyard, and his banner over me is love.

5“Refresh me with raisin cakes, spread out apricots for me, for I
am faint with love. 6His left hand is under my head, and his
right hand caresses me.

7“I earnestly urge you all, daughters of Jerusalem, by the gazelles or by the deer of the field, do not arouse, do not stir up sexual desire until love can take pleasure in it.”

Commentary

There’s something electric about new love. You’ve seen it—maybe you’ve experienced it. The young man or woman who can’t stop talking about their beloved. They are annoying in the best possible way. Every conversation somehow circles back to “he said” or “she did.” Their relatives roll their eyes. Their friends smile patiently. It’s the first bloom of love, and it’s both wonderful and exhausting for everyone around them.

That’s exactly what new Christians are like. When someone first encounters Jesus, truly encounters him and falls in love with him, they become some of the most joyfully annoying people on the planet. They want to tell everyone. They can’t help themselves. Their unsaved relatives often bear the brunt of it, which is actually wonderful—it's part of the process. The new believer is experiencing the first bloom of love with Jesus Christ, and they are enamored with this Savior who did something amazing for them.

The Song of Songs opens in exactly this place—the place of new, passionate, all-consuming love. It doesn't start gently. Verse one names Solomon as author, and then the first poem begins.

Shulammite:

"Let him kiss me with the kisses from his mouth—for your lovemaking is sweeter than wine. Your lotions have an aromatic fragrance, your name is oil poured from one vessel to another, therefore the young women love you. Carry me off after you, let us run!"

"The king brought me to his bedroom." (1:2-4a)

The book starts in high gear. This is the Shulammite speaking—Solomon's bride—and she's not being coy. She wants kisses. She wants sexual intimacy. She wants to be alone with her beloved. She doesn't just want to be alone, she wants to be involved in the most intimate of marital behaviors, lovemaking.

Think about what she says: "*Your lovemaking is sweeter than wine.*" While most translations of this verse coyly translate it as, "Your love" is sweeter than wine, those translations are softening the meaning of this verse. We can see the meaning of the verb more clearly communicated in Ezekiel 16:8, "*I passed by you and looked, and significantly, you were at the age for sexual intimacy . . .*" The verb isn't just about feelings of love, it refers to the sexual intimacy that occurs between a husband and wife. When the Shulammite says that Solomon's lovemaking is sweeter than wine, she is saying that their times of sexual intimacy are wonderful. Wine represents joy, celebration, the goodness of life. But the love she's experiencing with Solomon, especially the physical love, surpasses all of that.

In the same way, when we first come to Christ, when we first experience his love for us—his willingness to die for us, his complete acceptance of us despite our failures—it's sweeter than anything this world offers. Every other pleasure pales in comparison.

The Shulammite continues: "*Your lotions have an aromatic fragrance.*" They both wore fragrances. They both worked to create an atmosphere when they were together. This is about more than just smelling good—it's about crafting an environment where love can flourish. When we gather to worship, we're doing the same thing. We're creating an atmosphere where we can encounter Jesus. The fragrances in the Song represent that atmosphere of worship, of prayer, of focused attention on the Beloved.

The Apostle Paul understood this. He wrote, "*But thanks be to God, who always reveals who we are in Christ, and makes the fragrance of the knowledge of Christ known through us in every place." (2 Corinthians 2:14).* We release a fragrance as God's people. When we teach about Christ, when we live for him, when we create space for his presence, we're releasing the knowledge of him into the world like perfume filling a room.

The Shulammite again, "*Your name is oil poured from one vessel to another.*" In that culture, if you wanted to purify oil, you'd pour it from one vessel to another repeatedly. The sediment would settle at the bottom, and you'd pour only the clear oil into the next container. Do it enough times, and the oil becomes crystal clear. She's saying his name is like that—it's pure, it's clear, everyone knows exactly who Solomon is when they hear his name. His reputation is without sediment.

How much more is that true of Jesus? When his name is spoken, when it's genuinely understood, it is pure light. There is no confusion, no muddiness. His character, his nature, his love—it is all clear as purified oil.

The Daughters of Jerusalem:

"Let us shout in exultation and delight in you; let us praise your lovemaking more than wine."

Shulammite:

"Rightly they love you." (1:4b)

The second half of verse 4 begins with commentary by a chorus, the daughters of Jerusalem, and the Shulammite affirms what they have said, "Rightly they love you." Here's something significant: the other young women love Solomon too. But they celebrate his relationship with the Shulammite. They are not jealous. They are not bitter. They say, in essence, "Let us praise your love for each other and the joy you find in each other's arms. This love is good and right, and we're happy for you."

In a real way, this is the body of Christ at its best. When we see someone stepping into a deeper relationship with Jesus, when we see God using someone powerfully, when we witness a brother or sister experiencing a breakthrough—we celebrate. We don't become envious. We don't say, "Why them and not me?" We say, "Look at that relationship! Look at what God is doing! This is wonderful!"

The daughters of Jerusalem appear throughout the Song of Songs as a chorus, a group that observes and responds to the relationship between Solomon and his bride. They represent the rest of God's people, the wider Church, those who witness and affirm the intimate relationships that individuals are having with Jesus.

Notice what they celebrate: "*Let us praise your lovemaking more than wine.*" They are not embarrassed by the intimacy. They don't try to tone it down or make it more respectable. They praise it. They recognize that this passionate, intimate love between the king and his bride is exactly what it should be.

The same is true in our relationship with Christ. Some people are uncomfortable with passionate worship, with deep emotional connection to Jesus, with the idea that we could be "in love" with our Savior. But the Song of Songs says that kind of intimacy is exactly what God wants with his people.

The Marks of the World

"I am dark but lovely, daughters of Jerusalem, like the tents of Kedar, like the tent curtains of Solomon. Do not look at me, for the sun has tanned me and my complexion is dark. The sons of my mother have been angry with me. They made me tend the vineyards, but my own vineyard I have not tended. [7]Tell me, you who my soul loves, where do you graze your flocks? Where do you give them rest at noon? For why should I be like one who veils herself by the flocks of your companions?" (1:5–7)

Now we see a bit of the bride's insecurity. She recognizes her imperfections. In that culture, a deep tan wasn't desirable—a light complexion was the ideal. If you were deeply tanned, it meant you'd been working outside. You were lower class. You hadn't been pampered and protected.

The Shulammite had been forced by her brothers to work in the family vineyards. They didn't think she was special. They didn't give her milk baths or keep her out of the sun. They said, "Go work just like everyone else." So she had the marks of hard labor on her—the dark complexion that revealed she wasn't from the pampered class.

"I am dark but lovely," she says. She owns both realities. Yes, she has these marks. Yes, she's imperfect. But she's also lovely. There's truth in both statements.

Every single one of us who comes to Christ has marks on us. We've been shaped by this world, by our families, by our circumstances, by our own choices. We look at ourselves and see the imperfections. We see where we fall short of the standard—and the standard is Jesus himself. We're supposed to be the bride of Christ, pure and without blemish, just like him. But when we look in the mirror, we see the tan. We see the evidence that this world has marked us.

Have you ever looked at yourself and wondered, "How could Jesus love me?" That's what the Shulammite is doing here. She's saying, "Don't look at me too closely. I'm not what you think. My brothers didn't value me. I had to work in the sun. My own vineyard —my own beauty, my own preparation—I haven't tended it."

Throughout the Song, "the vineyard" often represents physical intimacy between the lovers. She's saying, "I haven't been able to tend to my own intimate preparation. I've been too busy working for others."

In spite of her insecurity, she still wishes to be seen by Solomon. In her culture, women wore veils when they were away from the protection of their family. But she wants to be seen by her husband. "Tell me, you who my soul loves, where do you graze your flocks? Where do you give them rest at noon? For why should I be like one who veils herself by the flocks of your companions?"

She presses through her insecurities (as must the Bride of Christ) and seeks to be unveiled so that he can see who she really is, even with her own feelings of imperfection.

Solomon's Response

"If you do not know by yourself, O loveliest of women, go out following the footprints of the flock and graze your young goats by the tents of the shepherds. My intimate companion, I liken you to a mare for the chariots of Pharaoh. Your cheeks are beautiful with jewelry, your neck with strings of pearls. We will make jewelry of gold for you studded with silver." (1:8-11)

Solomon's response to her insecurity is perfect. First, he tells her how to find him so that she can be in his presence: "Follow the footprints. Follow those who have gone before." All she needs to do is follow the ones who already know the way.

This is a picture of Christian discipleship. We don't find Jesus by just sitting alone with our Bible, confused and isolated. We follow those who have walked the path before us. We gather with other believers. We learn from those who are further along in their faith. We follow the footprints that lead to where Jesus is.

Note that Solomon doesn't just give her directions. He affirms her beauty. She has shared some insecurity about her appearance, and Solomon responds with lavish praise of her beauty.

Some of Solomon's compliments don't translate well into our culture. "I liken you to a mare for the chariots of Pharaoh" isn't something that would excite most women today. We'd probably be offended if someone compared us to a horse. But in that culture, Pharaoh's horses were the most magnificent, best-bred, most beautifully adorned animals you could imagine. It was a supreme compliment.

The point isn't the specific comparison. The point is that Solomon is saying, "I see you. I see your beauty. And I'm going to make you even more beautiful. Your cheeks are beautiful with jewelry, your neck with strings of pearls. We will make jewelry of gold for you studded with silver."

He is saying, "Don't worry about the marks of the world on you. I'm going to adorn you. I'm going to make you beautiful. Yes, you have imperfections, but we're going to deal with those together. I'm going to cover you with beauty."

This is exactly what Jesus does for us. He doesn't deny our imperfections. He doesn't pretend we don't have marks from this world. But he covers us. He adorns us. He works with us to remove the foothold that sin has in our lives. He doesn't do it all at once—that would crush us. He does it progressively, dealing with one area at a time, all while covering the rest with his grace.

Think about it, God puts the covering of grace on the imperfections of our sin. Everything is covered by grace when we first come to him. Then he starts working on specific issues, one at a time. When one issue is dealt with and Satan no longer has that foothold, God graciously shows us the next area he wants to work on. He often does that by taking the covering of restraining grace off that area, so we can see it clearly and address it.

This can be a difficult experience. We think we're backsliding when this happens. "Why am I suddenly struggling with this? I thought I was past this!" But actually, it's a sign of progress. God has already dealt with something else, and now he is ready to work on the next thing. That's not falling away—that's being promoted in your sanctification.

Solomon's response to his bride's insecurity is to affirm her, to give her the path to find him, and to promise that he will make her even more beautiful. That's Jesus' response to us every single time we come to him with our imperfections.

Creating Atmosphere

"When the king was on his couch, my perfumed lotion released its fragrance. My lover is a sachet of myrrh to me, spending the night between my breasts. My lover is a cluster of henna in the vineyards of En Gedi." (1:12-14)

The Shulammite is preparing herself. She's wearing perfumed lotions so that when Solomon reclines on his couch, the fragrance reaches him. She wants him to smell her presence before he even sees her. She's creating atmosphere.

A sachet of myrrh is a small pouch of this extremely expensive perfume. Myrrh was one of the gifts the Magi brought to Jesus—gold, frankincense, and myrrh. Throughout the Song, these fragrances appear, and we can't help but see hints of the incarnation, hints that this is about more than just Solomon and his bride.

But at this level, it's about creating the right environment for intimacy. She's not passive in this relationship. She's actively working to make her presence pleasant to her husband. He's doing the same—he smells good to her too, and as a result, she looks forward to some very intimate things when they are together.

This matters for our relationship with Christ. We create atmosphere through worship, through prayer, through our attitudes. When we come to worship on Sunday morning, are we creating an atmosphere where we can encounter Jesus? Or are we distracted, checking our phones, greeting everyone who walks in late, multitasking in the presence of God?

It is clear that it is important to create an atmosphere of worship in our lives. However, just as it would be inappropriate for someone to devise a list or rules for husbands and wives to follow in their lovemaking, so also we must be careful not to make many rules or guidelines for how others approach Jesus. It is about the spontaneity and relationship. But as we learn what our Savior appreciates, we can approach him in ways that honor him without stealing the freedom we need to truly respond to him.

Mutual Appreciation

Solomon speaks: "*Look how beautiful you are, my intimate companion, how beautiful you are. Your eyes are doves." (1:15)*

The Shulammite responds:

"Look how handsome you are, my lover, and so pleasant. Truly our bed is fresh and green. The timber work of our house is cedar. Our rafters are juniper." (1:16-17)

They are appreciating each other. Back and forth, affirmation flows between them. This is vital in any relationship. Husbands and wives who stop affirming each other, who stop noticing beauty in one another, who stop expressing appreciation—their relationships wither.

But this is also vital in our relationship with Christ. We need to express our love for him. We need to tell him we appreciate him. Worship isn't just about receiving from God—it's about giving back to him, telling him how wonderful he is, how much we love him.

Notice: "Truly our bed is fresh and green." They are committed to keeping the relationship vibrant. The bed being "fresh and green" means it's alive, it's growing, it's not stale or dead. The house is well-built—cedar timber work, juniper rafters. These are expensive, durable materials. They are saying, "We're building something that will last, and we're keeping it fresh and alive."

That's the goal for every husband and wife, and the goal of every believer: keep the relationship fresh and green. Don't let it become routine or dead. Keep pursuing. Keep creating atmosphere. Keep expressing love.

The Rose of Sharon

The Shulammite: "*I am the rose of Sharon, a lily of the valleys." (2:1)*

Solomon: "*As a lily between the thorns, so my intimate companion is among the daughters of Jerusalem." (2:2)*

The Shulammite continues: "*As an apricot among the trees of the woodlands, so my lover is among the sons of Jerusalem. I delighted greatly and rested in his shade, and his fruit was sweet to my taste."(2:3)*

This is the only place in Scripture where someone is called "the rose of Sharon." In Hebrew, it's clearly the bride speaking—feminine endings make that certain. So when we sing about Christ being the Rose of Sharon, we're actually applying the bride's words to the Bridegroom. That has come to us through tradition more than through Scripture. But it's not inappropriate—in fact, it's beautiful. Because the bride of Christ should look like the Bridegroom, should reflect his character, should be so much like him that his attributes become hers.

But here the Shulammite is saying, "I'm singular. I'm unique. I'm the rose of Sharon, a lily of the valleys." She recognizes that she's special, that she's been created by God for a purpose.

Solomon agrees, but he puts it even more strongly: "You're a lily among thorns." He's saying all the other daughters of Jerusalem are thorns compared to her. That might not be very complimentary to the other women, but from Solomon's perspective, there is only one who matters. There are lots of potential relationships out there, and every time he reaches for them, he gets hurt (the thorns). But with the Shulammite, there's no hurt, no pain—just beauty, just the lily.

She returns the compliment: "You are an apricot tree among the forest." Everyone else is just a tree. "You are the one with sweet fruit." She's enjoying him, resting in his shade, tasting his fruit. This is intimate language, poetic language, the language of a woman who is deeply in love and deeply satisfied in her relationship.

This is what our relationship with Christ should feel like. We should be able to say, "I rest in his shade. His fruit is sweet to my taste. I delight greatly in him." This is not because we are after an experience, but because we are in genuine relationship with the One who loves us most.

His Banner Over Me

"He brought me to the vineyard, and his banner over me is love. Refresh me with raisin cakes. Spread out apricots for me, for I am faint with love. His left hand is under my head, and his right hand caresses me." (2:4-6)

The song, "His banner over me is love," came from this very intimate verse. The vineyard, remember, represents times of physical intimacy between the lovers. He's brought her to a place of deep connection, and his banner—his flag, his declaration, his proclamation—over her is love.

She is overwhelmed. "I am faint with love." She needs to be refreshed, to be strengthened. In the same way, when the presence of God shows up in power, sometimes it's hard to stand. Sometimes we need to be fed, strengthened, helped to be able to handle the intensity of his presence.

The imagery of his left hand under her head and his right hand caressing her is intimate. This is a husband and wife in close intimate embrace. But it's also a picture of how Christ holds us, supports us, caresses us with his love.

Don't Awaken Love Before the Time

"I earnestly urge you, all daughters of Jerusalem, by the gazelles or by the deer of the field, do not arouse, do not stir up sexual desire until love can take pleasure in it." (2:7)

This warning appears three times in the Song of Songs. It is that important. On the surface, it's saying what every wise parent tells their children: don't awaken sexual desire before you're ready to handle it in the context of marriage. Don't start something you can't finish appropriately. Don't play with fire.

But there is a deeper meaning here for our relationship with Christ. Don't pursue experiences of God's presence before you are ready to handle them maturely. Don't become addicted to the feeling of his presence without developing your character through studying his Word, knowing his ways, growing in righteousness.

I saw the reason for this warning during the refreshing that happened in the mid-1990s. God's presence was coming into worship services in powerful ways. People were experiencing the power of God in profound ways. There was laughter, there was weeping, there was a tangible experience of his presence.

During this time, I watched as some new believers got addicted to that experience. They chased it. They went from meeting to meeting, looking for the next touch, the next fall, the next experience.

Of course, I applauded their hunger for God and his presence. But then I noticed something: some were not growing. They were not studying Scripture. They were not developing character. They were not learning to serve. They became spiritual adrenaline junkies, and I watched shipwreck after shipwreck as their lives fell apart because they had awakened intimate desire before they were ready to handle it maturely.

This is a solemn warning. God wants to give us profound experiences of his presence. But he also wants us to grow up. He wants us to be fed with teaching, with the Word, with understanding of who he is. Like newborn babes, we should crave pure spiritual milk so that we grow up in our salvation (cf. 1 Peter 2:2). Then, when he entrusts us with deeper experiences, we won't let those experiences baptize our bad behavior. We won't use them as an excuse to avoid the character development he is working in us.

Don't awaken intimate desire until love can take pleasure in it. Don't pursue the experience of God until you're pursuing the character of God. Both are important. Both are necessary. But there's an order, a timing, a maturity that needs to develop.

The First Bloom

This is the first bloom of love. It's passionate, it's exciting, it's all-consuming. Solomon and the Shulammite are enamored with each other. They are creating atmosphere, affirming one another, pursuing intimacy, delighting in each other's presence.

This is exactly what happens when someone first comes to Christ. There's that first blush of salvation, that fresh encounter with the One who loved them enough to die for them. They can't stop talking about him. They are annoying to their unsaved relatives and wonderful to watch.

But the first bloom of love, as beautiful as it is, isn't the end goal. It's the beginning. The goal is a mature love, a tested love, a love that has survived trials and grown deeper. The goal is a bride who reflects her husband's best qualities, not just someone who has emotional experiences with him.

We're about to watch the relationship between Solomon and the Shulammite be tested. We're going to see bumps in the road. We're going to watch the bride make mistakes and face consequences. Through it all, we're going to see Solomon's relentless pursuit of his bride, and by extension, God's relentless pursuit of his people as he works to bring forth a mature bride.

But for now, we celebrate the first bloom. We celebrate the beauty of new love, the joy of fresh encounter, the passion of two hearts discovering each other. This is how every relationship with Jesus should begin—with wonder, with delight, with the recognition that nothing in this world is sweeter than his love.

2
SPRINGTIME INVITATION

Song of Songs Chapter Two (Verses 8-17)

The Shulammite

8"The voice of my lover! Look, he is coming, leaping over the
mountains, bounding over the hills. 9My lover is like a
gazelle or a youthful stag among the stags. Look, he is
standing behind our wall. He is watching through the
windows. He is looking through the lattice.

10"My lover responds to me and says,"

Solomon

" 'Arise, my intimate companion, my beautiful one, and come.
11For look, the winter has passed, the rain has finished and
gone by. 12The blossoms have appeared in the land, a time
for singing has arrived. The voice of the turtledove is heard
in our land. 13The fig tree has brought forth her figs, and the
blossoms of the vines have released their sweet smell. Arise,
come my intimate lover, my beautiful one, and come. 14My
dove in the clefts of the rock, in the shelter of the cliff, show
me your figure, let me hear your voice. For your voice is
sweet and your figure is lovely.' "

The Shulammite

15"Hold the foxes for us, the young foxes that are ruining the vineyards, and our vineyards are in blossom. 16My lover is mine and I am his; he grazes among the lilies 17until the day begins and the shadows flee. Move around, my lover, be like a gazelle, or a youthful stag upon the mountains by my cleavage.[2]"

Commentary

One Sunday morning, our worship pastor sent me a picture. It was taken in his backyard that very morning—a mangy, sickly-looking fox wandering around where foxes don't typically appear. He and his wife had never seen a fox in their yard before. Nobody that I knew had.

On that Sunday morning I was about to preach on Song of Songs 2:15, "*Hold the foxes for us, the young foxes that are ruining the vineyards.*" When I saw that picture, I knew immediately what was happening. God was confirming his word. He was saying, "Pay attention to this. This message about the foxes—the distractions that ruin your intimacy with me—this is not just ancient poetry. This is for you, for your congregation, for this moment."

I sent the picture to the prophet who had given me this assignment. His response: "(This) . . . is an affirmation of the message you're bringing today." Yes. It absolutely was.

The sovereign God of the universe sent a fox into our worship pastor's backyard on the exact morning I was preaching about foxes ruining the vineyard. He wanted us to get the message. He wanted us to understand that this message really is from him for his people at this time.

---

2 Because of the overtly sexual nature of this passage, and the fact that grazing among the lilies refers to lovemaking, valley is best translated "cleavage" (so also NASB in footnote)

Do not miss this: God is speaking to us about distractions, about the little things that can destroy our intimacy with him. And he cares enough to send a fox to make sure we pay attention.

The Voice of My Lover

"The voice of my lover. Look, he is coming, leaping over the mountains, bounding over the hills. My lover is like a gazelle or a youthful stag among the stags. Look, he is standing behind our wall. He is watching through the windows. He is looking through the lattice." (2:8–9)

The Shulammite's ear is tuned to her lover's voice. She hears him coming from a distance, and she's excited. In her mind, she pictures him bounding toward her with youthful vigor, leaping over mountains in his eagerness to get to her.

This is John 10:27 illustrated: "*My sheep have come to know my voice. I know them and they follow me.*"

We can be walking down the road, and suddenly we hear the voice of Jesus. He speaks little bits into our ears—things that seem like nothing but are never nothing because it is him. It's the God of the universe, the sovereign King, taking time to whisper to us. As we grow in our relationship with him, we learn to discern his voice from all the other voices that fill our heads.

There are a lot of voices. There's our own internal dialogue, of course, but the spiritual airwaves are full too. The second heaven—the realm between us and God's throne—is crowded with voices. Satan and his demons are broadcasting constantly. If you think every voice you hear is God, you're going to end up twisted into a pretzel.

We have to get good at discerning his voice. How do we do that? Is what you're hearing in line with Scripture? That's the number one test. Does it contradict God's revealed character and commands? If so, it's not him.

Satan's voices condemn relentlessly. They pile on every failure, every mistake, every weakness. They tell you you're worthless, hopeless, that God is done with you. When you hear someone say,

"God told me to do this," and they do something absolutely wicked and awful that appalls the world, you know it wasn't God. They heard a demonic voice and called it God.

But Jesus' voice brings conviction with hope. Yes, he points out what needs to change, but he only shows you what he is ready to help you fix. He doesn't pile everything on you at once. He brings hope for change, not hopeless condemnation.

The Holy Spirit is called the Helper, but that word also means Encourager. God is constantly encouraging us because the world beats us down and Satan accuses us relentlessly. We need encouragement to counter the lies.

So the Shulammite recognizes Solomon's voice, and she's thrilled. He's coming to her with energy and passion, bounding toward her like a young stag. This is Jesus eager to spend time with his Church and bring his encouragement.

Arise, My Love

"My lover responds to me, 'Arise, my intimate companion, my beautiful one, and come. For look, the winter has passed. The rain has finished and gone by. The blossoms have appeared in the land. It's a time for singing has arrived. The voice of the turtle dove is heard in our land. The fig tree has brought forth her figs, and the blossoms of the vines have released their sweet smell.' " (2:10–13a)

What a vivid picture of springtime! Solomon is standing at the lattice, looking in at his bride, and he is painting this beautiful picture of what's waiting outside. The winter is over. The rain has stopped. Flowers are blooming. Birds are singing. The fig tree has fruit. The vines are fragrant.

He is saying, "Come out with me. Come enjoy this beautiful season. Let's experience this together."

There's nothing quite like springtime for love. In virtually every culture, spring represents new beginnings, fresh starts, the awakening of life after dormancy. Solomon is inviting the Shulammite to step out of the house and into this glorious season with him.

This is also Jesus inviting us to come and spend time with him. He's always calling us to "come away" with him, to step out of our routines and into his presence. Sometimes he calls us in the night seasons—inconvenient times when we'd rather sleep. Sometimes he calls us when we're busy with other things. But he is always calling, always inviting, always saying, "Come be with me."

"Arise, come, my intimate lover, my beautiful one, and come, my dove in the clefts of the rocks, in the shelter of the cliff, show me your figure, let me hear your voice, for your voice is sweet and your figure is lovely." (2:13b-14)

In essence, he is saying, "Come out into the light. Stop hiding. Let me see you and hear you."

When the Shulammite is in the house, she's like a dove hiding in the cleft of a rock—in shadows, in shelter. Solomon wants her to come out into the sunlight where he can enjoy her fully. He wants to hear her voice. Like any husband, he wants to enjoy her beauty.

Jesus says the same to us. Stop hiding. Come out into the light. Let me see you. Let me hear your voice. And he showers us with words of love and affirmation so we will have the courage to keep coming to him, keep stepping out into his presence.

His desire is to see his fruit developing in our lives. He said, *"I am the vine, you are the branches . . . apart from me you can do nothing" (John 15:5).* But if we're connected to him, we're going to bear fruit all our lives. The fruit of our relationship with Jesus—that's what he wants to see growing.

Hold the Foxes

"Hold the foxes for us, the young foxes that are ruining the vineyards, and our vineyards are in blossom." (2:15)

Now we are at the vineyard—the place of intimacy between them. The Shulammite says something that is vitally important: "Hold the foxes."

Foxes are small. They are not bears or lions that obviously threaten everything. They are little. But if you have a vineyard, you don't want foxes. They'll destroy your vines. They'll eat your grapes. They'll ruin what you're trying to grow.

The foxes are the distractions that ruin the moments.

Think about all the things that can distract a married couple from each other. The cell phone buzzing during dinner. The television always on in the background. Work stress brought home. Kids' activities that consume every evening. None of these things are evil in themselves, but they are foxes—small distractions that, if left unchecked, will destroy the vineyard of intimacy.

My wife Dawn and I learned this years ago. When we go out to eat together, before the waitress comes, we check whatever we need to check on our phones, and then we put them away. During the meal, we're present with each other. That's the whole point of going out—to spend time together, to keep our relationship fresh and green. We can eat food at home. We go to a restaurant to focus on each other without distractions.

The same is true in our relationship with Jesus. There are so many distractions. Our phones are the obvious ones—constant notifications, texts, emails, social media. But there are more subtle foxes too.

Let me give you a specific example from our church gatherings. Worship starts, and some people come in five or ten minutes late. That's fine—life happens. But then they start greeting everyone. They are hugging people, catching up, asking how the week was—and meanwhile, worship is happening. Jesus is present. The Holy Spirit is moving. And people are being pulled right out of their connection with him.

I have mentioned this on occasion. I've said, "Listen, the most important thing happening right now is connecting with Jesus. When you interrupt people during worship, you're taking them away from the most important relationship they have. You can greet each other before worship starts or after it ends, but during worship, let's focus on him."

That's holding the foxes. That's refusing to let small distractions destroy the intimacy we're cultivating with Jesus.

We live in a multitasking world. Our devices make certain of that. But don't multitask in the presence of God. Hold those types of foxes. When God is speaking, when his presence is manifest, that becomes the priority. Everything else can wait.

Now, remember the picture I mentioned at the beginning of this chapter? Our worship leader's fox? God sent that fox *to our worship leader* on the exact morning I was preaching this passage to drive home the point. He wants us to get it. He wants us to understand that this isn't just ancient poetry or nice spiritual principles. This is a now word for all of us. Do not let the little foxes ruin your vineyard. Don't let distractions pull you away from the most important relationship you have. Don't let the urgent crowd out the essential. Don't let the good become the enemy of the best.

When Jesus knocks at your door, when he invites you into his presence, when he is calling you to come away with him—hold the foxes. Push aside the distractions. Turn off the phone. Close the laptop. Tell the kids to wait. Say, "No" to whatever is trying to interrupt.

Because the King is calling.

My Lover Is Mine

"My lover is mine and I am his. He grazes among the lilies until the day begins and the shadows flee. Move around, my lover, be like a gazelle, or a youthful stag upon the mountains by my cleavage." (2:16)

This is the Shulammite's declaration of the relationship. She belongs to him, and he belongs to her. It's mutual possession, mutual delight, mutual commitment. She is delighted that he is grazing among the lilies, a euphemism that means that they are enjoying sexual pleasure with each other. She enjoys the fact that Solomon enjoys her breasts and wants him to spend time moving around them. The Shulammite is completely sold out to this relationship and the physical intimacies of love.

We can say the same thing the Shulammite says about our relationship with Jesus. He is ours, and we are his. We have a relationship with the God of the universe. We're connected to him like a branch to a vine. He's the vine, we're the branches, and we have a life-relationship with him that needs to continue growing so more life can flow through us into the world.

We can get excited about that. Some people wake up in the morning thinking, "Oh no, another day." But we can wake up thinking, "I get to connect with the Lord today. I wonder if he will give me a dream tonight. I wonder what he will say to me tomorrow. I wonder how he will speak."

Yes, I'm just like everyone else—I don't always want to be awakened at 3 a.m. But when the Lord speaks, when he gives a dream or a word or an insight, it's worth being awakened for it. He can make up the sleep. He can cover us. But the moment when he is speaking—that's the moment that matters.

This is what the Shulammite understands. She's saying, "I don't want the foxes to distract us. I want to be fully present with you. You're mine and I'm yours, and I want to enjoy every moment of this relationship."

That should be our heart cry. Jesus, you're mine and I'm yours. I don't want anything to distract me from you. I want to be fully present. I want to hear your voice. I want to respond when you call. I want our relationship to be the priority above everything else.

The Cost of Distraction

There is a cost to letting the foxes run wild in our vineyards. We see it all around us in the church today. Churches that have settled for good meetings without the Holy Spirit, Christians who have made their relationship with Jesus routine—daily devotions that feel like checking a box, worship that's more about musical preference than encountering God, prayers that are rote repetitions rather than real conversations.

The vineyard withers when the foxes aren't held back.

Here's what's sobering: Jesus is patient. He keeps knocking. He keeps inviting. But he also has other places to go, other people who will respond to his invitation. We will see this dynamic develop more fully in coming chapters, but the hint is already here.

Solomon is inviting the Shulammite to come enjoy springtime with him. Will she respond? Will she push aside the distractions and step into the moment with him? Or will she let the foxes keep her attention?

The same question confronts us constantly. Jesus is inviting us into his presence. He's showing us the beauty of relationship with him. He's calling us to come away, to spend time, to let him see and hear us. Will we respond? Will we hold back the foxes? Or will we let a thousand small distractions keep us from the One who loves us most?

Following the Footprints

Remember what Solomon told his bride earlier: *"If you do not know by yourself, O loveliest of women, go out following the footprints of the flock." (1:8)*

This is extremely important. We don't find Jesus by sitting alone, confused and isolated. We follow those who have gone before us. We gather with other believers. We learn from those further along in their faith. We follow the footprints that lead to where Jesus is.

This is why church matters. This is why gathering together matters. Not because a building is magic or because Sunday morning is somehow more holy than Tuesday afternoon, but because when we gather, we follow the footprints together. We help each other find Jesus. We encourage each other to hold back the foxes. We create an atmosphere where his presence can be experienced corporately.

Some people say, "I don't need church. I can worship God on my own." Yes, you can worship God on your own. You should worship God on your own. But you also need the gathered community. You need to follow the footprints of those who've gone before. You need to be encouraged when you're weak and to encourage others when they are weak. You need to hear voices other than your own saying, "Yes, this is Jesus. Yes, this is his voice. Yes, this is worth pursuing."

The Shulammite didn't find Solomon by wandering aimlessly. She followed the path that others had forged. She went to where the flock gathered. There she found him.

We do the same. We follow the footprints. We gather together. We help each other hold back the foxes. Together, we encounter the One who's been calling us all along.

Springtime is for Love

There's a reason Solomon issues his invitation in springtime. After winter—after dormancy, after barrenness, after cold and darkness—spring bursts forth with life and color and warmth. It's the season of new beginnings, of fresh starts, of life awakening.

Many of us are coming out of winter seasons. Maybe your relationship with Jesus has felt cold or distant. Maybe the heavens have felt closed. Maybe your prayers have seemed to bounce off the ceiling. That's winter.

But Jesus is inviting you into spring. He's saying, "The winter has passed. The rain is over. Come out with me. Let's experience this new season together."

Don't miss the invitation because of the foxes. Don't let distractions keep you in the house when Jesus is calling you outside. Don't let the small things rob you of the intimacy he is offering.

Hold the foxes. Push them back. Say no to the distractions. Step out into the springtime with Jesus.

He is calling. He's inviting. He's standing at the lattice, looking in, painting pictures of the beauty that's waiting if you'll just come away with him.

The voice of your Lover is calling. The blossoms have appeared. The time for singing has arrived. The vineyards are in bloom.

Hold the foxes, and go to him.

3
THE TEST OF ABSENCE

Song of Songs Chapter Three (Verses 1-5)

The Shulammite

1“Upon my bed at night, I sought him whom my soul loves. I
sought him but did not find him. 2Let me arise now and
walk around in the city, in the streets and in the plazas. Let
me seek the one my soul loves. I sought him but did not
find him. 3Those who keep watch doing their rounds in the
city found me. I asked, ’Have you seen the one whom my
soul loves?’

4“A moment after I passed by them, I found the one whom my
soul loves. I held him and did not stop until I had brought
him to the house of my mother, and to the room of the one
who conceived me.

5“I earnestly urge you all, daughters of Jerusalem, by the
gazelles or by the deer of the field, do not arouse, do not stir
up sexual desire until love can take pleasure in it.”

Commentary

The truth is that in our relationships, every day may not necessarily feel like springtime. Every moment is not filled with the sense of presence and connection. Sometimes, despite our best efforts, we can't seem to find the one we love. We search, we call out, but there's only silence.

This is the test of absence, and it's one of the most difficult tests we face in our relationship with Jesus.

Seeking in the Night

"Upon my bed at night, I sought him whom my soul loves. I sought him, but did not find him. Let me arise now and walk around in the city, in the streets and in the plazas. Let me seek the one my soul loves. I sought him, but did not find him." (3:1-2)

This is a new scene, a new poem in the collection. The Shulammite is in bed, but she is not deeply asleep. Her heart is awake, alert, waiting. She's expecting her lover to come. But he doesn't.

So she lies there in the darkness, seeking him. When he doesn't appear, she makes a decision: "Let me arise. Let me go look for him." She doesn't stay passive. She doesn't just accept his absence. She pursues.

This is the test of absence. Will she keep pursuing even when he is not immediately present? Will she search for him even when it's inconvenient, even when it means going out into the night, even when she doesn't know where to find him?

In our relationship with Jesus, we all face seasons like this; times when our devotions feel dry as dust; times when worship doesn't connect the way it usually does; times when we pray and the heavens feel silent; times when we seek him and don't immediately sense his presence.

Those are wilderness times, desert times, absence times.

They are tests. Will we keep pursuing him even when we don't feel his presence? Will we keep seeking even when he seems distant? Will we give up and say, "Well, if God doesn't want to be with me, I don't want to be with him either"? Or will we press through, knowing that he is there even when we can't sense him?

The Shulammite presses through. She gets up. She goes out into the city to search. Notice what happens.

The Watchmen

"Those who keep watch doing their rounds in the city found me. I asked, have you seen the one whom my soul loves?" (3:3)

The watchmen of the city find her. These are the guards, the protectors, the ones who patrol at night to keep order. They let her pass. They don't question her. They don't stop her. When she explains that she's looking for her lover, they give her a pass.

This is significant because later in the Song, she'll encounter these same watchmen again under very different circumstances. But for now, in this first test of absence, there's grace. The opposition isn't overwhelming. She's allowed to search.

"A moment after I passed by them, I found the one whom my soul loves. I held him and did not stop until I had brought him to the house of my mother and to the room of the one who conceived me." (3:4)

She finds him! Just after she passes the watchmen, she finds Solomon. She doesn't let him go. She holds him and brings him to a place where they can be intimate together.

The scene that started with her alone in bed ends with them together in a private place. She pursued, and she found. Her persistence paid off. Her refusal to accept his absence brought them back together.

This is what God wants to see in us. When we can't sense his presence, do we give up? Or do we press through? When our devotions feel dry, do we skip them? Or do we keep showing up, keep seeking, keep pursuing?

Drawing near to God is a command, not just a suggestion. James 4:8 says, *"Draw near to God and he will draw near to you."* The implication is clear: if we're not sensing his nearness, it's because we're not drawing near as we should.

This doesn't mean God is playing games with us. It means he is testing and developing our commitment. He's asking, "Do you want me enough to pursue me even when you don't feel me?"

The Warning Repeated

"I earnestly urge you all, daughters of Jerusalem, do not arouse, do not stir up intimate desire until love can take pleasure in it." (3:5)

This is the second time we've heard this warning, and it won't be the last. The Shulammite has just been through an experience of absence and pursuit. She's learned something about commitment, about pressing through, about not giving up when connection isn't immediate.

When she presses through and restores sexual intimacy, she once again warns the other women: Don't step into deep intimacy until you're ready to commit. Don't awaken these desires until you're prepared to follow through even when it's difficult.

For us, this means: Don't pursue deep experiences of God's presence if you're not willing to develop the character and commitment that sustains you when those experiences fade. Don't chase the feeling of his presence while neglecting the discipline of knowing his Word. Don't seek the mountaintop experiences while avoiding the valley work of obedience and faithfulness.

God wants to give us profound encounters with him. But he also wants us to be mature enough to handle them. He does not want us to become dependent on the feeling while neglecting the relationship.

The test of absence is designed to build that maturity. It's designed to show us whether we're pursuing Jesus himself or just pursuing an experience. Are we seeking the Giver or just the gifts? Are we in love with him or in love with how he makes us feel?

Calculating the Cost

Jesus spoke about this very thing. In Luke 14:27-30, he said:

"Whoever does not carry his own cross and come after me is not able to be my disciple. For who from among you wanting to build a watchtower doesn't first sit down and calculate what it will cost to see if he has enough to finish it? He does this so that he does not lay the foundation only to find he does not have the ability to complete it. When everyone sees it, they will begin to mock him and say, 'This man began to build but did not have the ability to complete it.'"

Jesus is saying, "Count the cost before you commit. Understand what you're getting into. Following me will cost you everything. Are you ready for that?"

I've told people to do this exercise: Sit down and write out everything you really want in life. Every dream, every goal, every desire. Write it all down. Then look at that list and ask yourself, "Am I willing to give all of this up for Jesus if he requires it?"

He might not require it. But are you willing if he does? That's counting the cost. That's making sure you're ready for the commitment before you awaken the intimate desire.

Because here's what happens if you don't, you start following Jesus with enthusiasm. You have great experiences. You feel his presence. Everything is wonderful. Then he asks you to give up something on your list. Maybe it's a relationship that's pulling you away from him. Maybe it's a career path that would compromise your integrity. Maybe it's a comfort or security to which you are clinging.

So you say, "No." You say, "Jesus, I love you, but not that much. I can't give that up."

And you shipwreck. You crash on the rocks because you awakened intimate desire before you were ready to pay the cost.

The Shulammite understands this now. She's been through the test of absence. She's learned that pursuing her lover sometimes means inconvenience, discomfort, persistence. She is saying to the other women, "Don't start this journey if you're not ready to see it through."

Why God Sometimes Seems Absent

God doesn't play games with us, but he does test us. He sometimes allows seasons of his apparent absence to teach us vital lessons:

First, to teach us that we need him. When we can always sense his presence, we can start taking it for granted. We can begin to think we've mastered the relationship, that we've figured out how to access him whenever we want. Seasons of absence remind us that he is sovereign, that we're dependent, that we need him desperately.

Second, to develop perseverance. James 1 tells us that the testing of our faith produces perseverance, and perseverance leads to maturity. If every prayer was answered immediately, if every worship time was emotionally powerful, if we always sensed his presence, we'd never develop the muscle of perseverance. The test of absence builds that muscle.

Third, to purify our motives. When we can't sense his presence, why are we still pursuing him? If it's for the feeling, we will give up. If it's for the benefits, we will get discouraged. But if it's for him—for Jesus himself, for relationship with the God who loves us—we will press through. Times of absence reveal and purify our motives.

Fourth, to teach us to walk by faith, not by sight (or feeling). Second Corinthians 5:7 says, "*We walk by faith, not by external appearances.*" Most of the Christian life is lived by faith, not by feeling. We believe he is there even when we can't sense him. We trust his promises even when circumstances contradict them. We keep obeying even when we're not feeling spiritual highs. That's maturity. That's faith. It's developed during times when his presence isn't obvious.

Pressing Through

The key to surviving the test of absence is simple: keep pursuing.

Don't stay in bed wondering where he is. Get up and go look for him. Read his Word even when it feels dry. Worship even when you don't feel like it. Pray even when the heavens feel like brass. Gather with other believers even when you'd rather stay home. Follow the footprints of those who've gone before. Ask the watchmen—ask mature believers, pastors, mentors—"Have you seen the One I love?"

Keep going. Keep seeking. Refuse to give up.

The Shulammite found her lover "a moment after" she passed the watchmen. Sometimes breakthrough is just on the other side of our next step of obedience. Sometimes we're about to give up right before we're about to break through.

I've seen this again and again in my own life and in the lives of others. Someone is in a dry season, questioning whether God is still there, wondering if they should quit. They are at the point of giving up. Then—breakthrough. God shows up. His presence becomes real again. The relationship is restored, deeper than before.

But if they had quit one step earlier, they would have missed it.

The Furnace of Affliction

Isaiah 48:10 says, "*Look, I have refined you, but not like silver; I have chosen you through the furnace of affliction.*"

The test of absence is a furnace. It's uncomfortable. It feels like affliction. We're crying out, "Where are you?" and hearing only silence. We're seeking and not immediately finding. We're wondering if we've done something wrong, if God is angry with us, if we've been abandoned.

But God says, "This is my way. This furnace has a purpose. I'm not testing you like silver—where the heat is so intense that the refiner quickly sees his reflection and knows the silver is pure. Rather, I'm using the furnace of affliction—allowing hard circumstances, allowing the sense of my absence—because that's what produces the steadily growing maturity that I choose to develop in you."

We don't like this. We'd much prefer for God to always feel close, for every prayer to get an immediate answer, for worship always to be emotionally powerful. We'd like Christianity to be a constant mountaintop experience.

But that's not how mature brides are formed. Mature brides are formed in the valley. They are formed in the wilderness. They are formed during seasons of absence when they have to choose to keep pursuing even though they don't feel anything.

From Test to Testimony

Here's the beautiful thing about the test of absence: when you pass through it, it becomes a testimony. When someone else hits a dry season, you can say, "I've been there. I know what it feels like. But let me tell you—he is still there even when you can't sense him. Keep pursuing. Keep seeking. Don't give up."

The Shulammite is able to encourage the daughters of Jerusalem because she's been through this test. She knows what it's like to lie in bed seeking her lover and not find him. She knows what it's like to get up and search through the city. She knows what it's like to ask for help. She knows what it's like to finally find him and hold onto him with everything in her.

Your tests become your testimony. Your wilderness becomes your message. The dry seasons you press through qualify you to encourage others who are in dry seasons.

But only if you press through. If you give up, if you quit when it gets hard, you don't have a testimony of faithfulness. You only have a story of starting well but not finishing.

A Moment of Transparency

I've been through many seasons of absence. Times when God felt far away. Times when my prayers seemed to bounce off the ceiling. Times when I wondered if I'd somehow disqualified myself from his presence.

I've been tempted during those times to just go through the motions. To maintain the appearance of relationship without the reality. To preach and teach from memory and study rather than from fresh encounter.

But I've learned that those wilderness times, those times of apparent absence, are some of the most critical times in my relationship with Jesus. Those are the times when I have to choose to pursue him because of who he is, not because of what I'm getting from him. Those are the times when faith becomes real, when commitment is tested, when love is proven.

Every single time I've pressed through, I've found him on the other side. Not always immediately. Sometimes it takes days or weeks. Sometimes the breakthrough comes in unexpected ways. But he always shows up. He always proves faithful. The test of absence always gives way to the joy of presence.

I'm telling you this because some of you are in that wilderness right now. You're seeking and not finding. You're calling out and hearing silence. You're wondering if something's wrong with you, if you've failed somehow, if God has moved on.

He hasn't. He's testing you. He's refining you. He's developing in you the kind of mature love that doesn't depend on feeling, the kind of commitment that perseveres through difficulty, the kind of faith that holds on even when circumstances say to let go.

Don't quit. Get up. Go search. Ask for help. Keep pursuing.

A moment after you pass the watchmen, you'll find him. When you do, hold on. Don't let go. Bring him to your private place and reconnect with him there.

The test of absence has a purpose. On the other side of it, you'll be stronger, more mature, more committed than ever before.

This is how brides are made. Not in constant comfort, but in tested commitment. Not in unbroken feelings of closeness, but in choosing to pursue even when he seems far away.

The Shulammite passed the test. She sought, she pursued, she found, she held on.

So should we.

4
VICTORY AND THE SEDAN CHAIR

Song of Songs Chapter Three (Verses 6-11)

The Daughters of Jerusalem

6"What is this coming up from the wilderness like columns of smoke perfumed with myrrh and frankincense, with all the scented spices of the traders? 7Look, it is the sedan chair of Solomon, sixty mighty men surround it of the mighty men of Israel. 8All of them are holding a sword, all are skilled in battle, each man with his sword on his thigh against the dread of the nights.

9"King Solomon has made for himself a sedan chair, from the trees of Lebanon. 10He made its posts of silver, its seat-back of gold, its seat of purple; its interior is inlaid with love by the daughters of Jerusalem. 11Go out, daughters of Zion, and look upon King Solomon with the nuptial crown with which his mother crowned him on the day of his wedding, on the day of his heart's elation."

Commentary

After the intimate scene of the bride pursuing and finding her lover in the night, we encounter something unexpected—a very public, very grand spectacle. The camera pulls back, if you will, and we see something coming up from the wilderness. Not two lovers in a private room, but a royal procession that catches everyone's attention.

The daughters of Jerusalem—those who have been observing this relationship all along—suddenly cry out with a question.

What Is This?

"What is this coming up from the wilderness like columns of smoke perfumed with myrrh and frankincense with all the scented spices of the traders?" (3:6)

Notice they don't ask "who" but "what." They are seeing something —a spectacle, a procession, something magnificent rising from the wilderness. It is surrounded by smoke, perfumed with myrrh and frankincense.

Now we need to pause here. Where else in Scripture do myrrh and frankincense appear together? Gold, frankincense, and myrrh—the gifts the Magi brought to Jesus. We've already seen gold mentioned throughout the Song in all the jewelry Solomon gives his bride. Now we have frankincense and myrrh appearing together, perfuming this procession from the wilderness.

This is intentional. Written a thousand years before Jesus was born, under the inspiration of the Holy Spirit, these hints are placed here so that when Christ came, when the Magi brought their gifts, when Jesus walked out of his own wilderness temptation victorious—we would begin to see the connections.

This isn't just about Solomon anymore. Or rather, Solomon is pointing beyond himself to the greater King, the true Prince of Peace, the real Bridegroom.

"Look, it is the sedan chair of Solomon. Sixty mighty men surround it of the mighty men of Israel. All of them are holding a sword. All are skilled in battle. Each man with his sword on his thigh against the dread of the night." (3:7–8)

Now we see clearly: it's Solomon's palanquin, his royal sedan chair, coming up from the wilderness. He is surrounded by sixty warriors—elite soldiers, skilled in battle, armed and ready.

This is a victory procession. Solomon has been in the wilderness, and he is emerging victorious. The smoke and perfume create an almost ethereal atmosphere. The warriors demonstrate his power and security. This is a king at the height of his glory, returning from conquest.

In a very real sense, this is also a picture of Christ coming out of the wilderness after his forty days of temptation. Satan had thrown everything at him—physical hunger, spiritual testing, the offer of worldly kingdoms. But Jesus emerged victorious, and he immediately stepped into his public ministry with power.

"Then the Accuser left him, and significantly, angels came and began to serve him" (Matthew 4:11). That's Jesus' victory procession from the wilderness.

The Sedan Chair

A sedan chair can be a massive, ornate structure carried by dozens of people, with the king seated inside, surrounded by attendants and guards. It's splendor on display. It's power visible to everyone. That type of sedan chair is meant to inspire awe and demonstrate authority.

However, a sedan chair can be much smaller and carried by fewer people. This is the type of sedan chair used in some cultures today when a bride is being carried in her own palanquin to the home of her husband. She's enclosed, somewhat hidden, but the procession itself is public and celebratory.

Solomon's sedan chair would have been somewhere between these —ornate, impressive, surrounded by warriors, coming up from the wilderness in a cloud of perfumed smoke. Everyone seeing it would have recognized that the king was coming. Victory has been won. Power is on display.

"King Solomon has made for himself a sedan chair from the trees of Lebanon. He made its posts of silver, its seat back of gold, its seat of purple, its interior is inlaid with love by the daughters of Jerusalem." (3:9-10)

The materials tell us about the care and cost involved. Cedar from Lebanon—the best, most expensive wood. Posts of silver. Seat back of gold. Purple fabric—the color of royalty, because purple dye was extraordinarily expensive. The interior? "Inlaid with love by the daughters of Jerusalem."

The people of God helped build this. They participated in creating the vehicle by which their king would travel. Their love was literally built into the structure.

Now let's transpose this to Christ and the Church. What was Jesus' vehicle during his three years of ministry? What carried him into the world to woo his bride?

His suffering and obedience.

That was his sedan chair. His perfect obedience to the Father, even unto death. His willingness to suffer on behalf of his people. His servant leadership that washed feet and touched lepers and welcomed sinners.

Who helped build that vehicle? The disciples. The women who supported his ministry. The people who received his teaching and passed it on. The daughters of Jerusalem—God's people—participated in creating the means by which Jesus wooed his bride.

After he ascended to heaven, the disciples continued the work. They took the message of the gospel to the ends of the earth. They built the Church. They helped construct the ongoing work of Christ in the world.

We're still doing that. Every time we share the gospel, every time we serve in Jesus' name, every time we make his love known—we're helping to build his sedan chair. We're participating in the means by which Jesus woos his bride in this generation.

The Nuptial Crown

"Go out, daughters of Zion, and look upon King Solomon with the nuptial crown with which his mother crowned him on the day of his wedding, on the day of his heart's elation." (3:11)

This is beautiful. The daughters of Zion—God's people—are invited to come out and look at their king. Not just any king, but their king on his wedding day, wearing the crown his mother gave him. Bathsheba crowned Solomon. It was a day of joy, a day when his heart was glad.

For us, this is an invitation to look at Jesus. To see him as he is—victorious, glorious, worthy of all praise. To recognize what he has done. To understand the lengths he went to in order to win us as his bride.

When did Jesus' heart experience the greatest elation? When he ascended on high and was able to take control of the Church, to rule all things on our behalf. When he saw that his suffering had accomplished its purpose—that a people would be redeemed, that a bride would be won, that he could work in and through us to produce fruit on his behalf.

He is working on our behalf all the time. Every moment, interceding for us, guiding us, protecting us, providing for us. His heart's elation is in his relationship with his bride.

We get to participate in that joy. When we understand who Jesus is and what he has done, when we see his victory and receive the benefit of it, when we recognize that all of this—the suffering, the obedience, the death, the resurrection—was for us, we join in the celebration.

That's what this passage is inviting us to do. To look at him. To see him. To tell others about him. To say, "Look at the King. Look at what he has done. Look at how he has won his bride."

Solomon as a Picture of the Messiah

We need to understand why Solomon appears so prominently in this love story. It's not accidental. Solomon was always intended to be a picture of the Messiah.

Remember the story: David wanted to build a temple for God. The prophet Nathan initially said, "Go ahead, do it." But that night, God spoke to Nathan and said, "Wait. Tell David I'm going to build a dynasty for him. One of his sons will build the temple."

That son was Solomon. He was a man of peace—his very name comes from the Hebrew word *shalom*, meaning peace. He was the one who built the temple, the dwelling place of God among his people. He was the wisest man who ever lived (until Jesus). He was fabulously wealthy. His reign was a golden age for Israel.

All of this pointed forward to the Messiah—to Jesus, the ultimate Son of David, the true Prince of Peace, the One who would build his temple in us, the One whose wisdom surpasses all understanding, the One who possesses all authority in heaven and earth.

So when the Holy Spirit inspired Solomon to write this love song, he wasn't just telling Solomon's story. He was telling Jesus' story. He was showing us what the Messiah's relationship with his people would look like.

Solomon's victory procession from the wilderness prefigures Christ's victory. Solomon's sedan chair, built with the help of the daughters of Jerusalem, prefigures the gospel work that Christ and his disciples would accomplish together. Solomon's wedding day, the day of his heart's elation, prefigures the joy Christ has in his relationship with his Church.

This is why Paul could write in Ephesians 5 about husbands and wives and then say, *"This is a great mystery; but I am speaking to Christ and to the Church" (Ephesians 5:32).* He understood that marriage—and specifically the marriage described in the Song of Songs—is a picture of something greater.

The Church's Role

Notice again that the daughters of Jerusalem participated in building Solomon's sedan chair. "Its interior is inlaid with love by the daughters of Jerusalem." They contributed. They helped. Their love was built into the vehicle.

This is significant: We have a role in Christ's ongoing work in the world.

Yes, Jesus accomplished our salvation. He finished the work on the cross. "It is finished," he said. There's nothing we can add to what he did to redeem us.

But he has given us the privilege of participating in the ongoing work of building his kingdom. We get to help. We get to contribute. Our love, our service, our gifts, our witness—it all becomes part of how Jesus makes himself known in the world.

Think about it. How do most people encounter Jesus today? Through his people. Through the Church. Through Christians who share the gospel, who demonstrate his love, who pray for the sick, who serve the poor, who create worship music, who write books, who preach sermons, who disciple new believers.

We're building his sedan chair. We're creating the means by which Jesus travels through this world and woos his bride.

That is an incredible privilege. It is also an incredible responsibility.

When we fail to represent him well, when we're judgmental or hypocritical or self-righteous, we damage the sedan chair. We make it harder for people to see Jesus clearly. We create obstacles instead of removing them.

But when we love well, when we serve humbly, when we speak truth with grace, when we demonstrate the character of Christ—we're adding to the beauty of the sedan chair. We're making it easier for people to see Jesus and be drawn to him.

The daughters of Jerusalem inlaid the interior with love. What are we adding? What are we contributing to the ongoing work of making Jesus known?

Coming Up From the Wilderness

There's one more crucial element here: this procession is coming *up from the wilderness.*

The wilderness is where testing happens. It's where Israel wandered for forty years, learning to trust God. It's where Jesus was tempted for forty days, proving his worthiness to be our Savior. It's where we go when we face trials and difficulties and seasons of apparent absence from God.

But the wilderness isn't the destination. It's the testing ground. The goal is to come *up* from it—to emerge victorious, stronger, more committed, more mature.

Solomon's sedan chair is coming up from the wilderness in victory. He's been tested. He's proven himself. Now he is returning in glory.

Jesus came up from the wilderness after his temptation and immediately began his public ministry. *"From that point, Jesus began to preach and say, 'Repent, for the Kingdom of the Heavens has drawn near'" (Matthew 4:17).* The wilderness tested him. The wilderness proved him. Then he emerged to do the work he was called to do.

The same pattern holds for us. We go through wilderness seasons. We face tests of absence, tests of inconvenience (which we will see in the next chapter), tests of faith and commitment. These aren't punishments. They are not signs that God is angry with us. They are the refining fire that produces mature brides.

When we come up from the wilderness—when we emerge on the other side, still faithful, still pursuing, still committed—we come up victorious. We come up stronger. We come up looking more like our Bridegroom.

The question isn't whether we will face wilderness seasons. We will. The question is: Will we come up from them? Or will we quit in the middle? Will we let the wilderness defeat us? Or will we let it refine us?

The Dread of the Nights

Notice one more detail about Solomon's warriors: *"Each man with his sword on his thigh against the dread of the nights."*

There are threats. There are dangers. Even in victory, even surrounded by warriors, there's an acknowledgment that the night holds terrors. This world is not safe. The enemy prowls around like a roaring lion, seeking whom he may devour.

But the warriors are ready. They are armed. They are skilled. They are protecting their king.

For us, this is spiritual warfare. We have an enemy who wants to destroy our relationship with Jesus. He wants to discourage us, distract us, deceive us. He wants to make us give up in the wilderness instead of coming up from it victorious.

But we're not defenseless. We have the armor of God. We have the sword of the Spirit, which is the Word of God. We have prayer. We have the authority Jesus has given us. We have the Holy Spirit dwelling in us.

We have each other. Just as Solomon was surrounded by sixty mighty men, we're surrounded by the body of Christ. We don't face the dread of the night alone. We have brothers and sisters who will stand with us, fight with us, encourage us when we're weak.

One of the reasons the Church matters so much is because we need each other in the battle. We need people who will hold up our arms when we're tired (like Aaron and Hur did for Moses). We need people who will speak truth to us when we're being deceived. We need people who will pray for us when we don't have the strength to pray for ourselves.

The warriors surrounding Solomon's sedan chair represent the community of faith that protects and supports the work of the King.

We're those warriors. We're called to stand against the dread of the night, not just for ourselves but for each other.

An Invitation to Look

"Go out, daughters of Zion, and look upon King Solomon."

This is an invitation. God is saying, "Come see your King. Come understand what he has done. Come appreciate his victory, his glory, his love for you."

Too many Christians never really look at Jesus. They believe in him as Savior. They know the basic facts of the gospel. But they never really *see* him. They never stand in awe of who he is and what he has accomplished. They never let the full weight of his love and sacrifice sink in.

This passage is calling us to look. To really look. To go out of our normal routines and perspectives and see Jesus as he truly is.

Look at his victory over sin and death.

Look at his obedience to the Father, even unto death on a cross.

Look at his resurrection power.

Look at his ascension and the authority given to him.

Look at his ongoing intercession for you.

Look at the sedan chair he built through his suffering so he could woo you as his bride.

Look at the crown—not of gold, but of thorns—that he wore for you.

Look at the day of his heart's elation—not just his ascension, but every day he sees fruit produced in your life, every day he sees you growing to look more like him, every day he sees his bride maturing.

When we really look at Jesus—when we see him as he is—everything changes. Our complaints seem petty. Our fears seem small. Our doubts seem foolish. Our excuses seem empty.

Because he is worth everything. He's worth the wilderness. He's worth the testing. He's worth the cost of discipleship.

The daughters of Jerusalem looked at Solomon and saw a king worth celebrating. We look at Jesus and see a King worth dying for.

No, more than that—a King worth *living* for.

This is the victory procession. This is the sedan chair coming up from the wilderness. This is the King in all his glory, wearing his nuptial crown, surrounded by his warriors, perfumed with myrrh and frankincense.

This is Jesus, victorious over sin and death, building his Church, wooing his bride, working on our behalf every moment of every day.

Look at him. Really look. Let your heart respond with worship, with commitment, with the determination to be the bride he deserves.

He is coming up from the wilderness victorious. We must be the bride he deserves.

5
WORDS OF AFFIRMATION AND INTIMACY

Song of Songs Chapter Four

Solomon

1"Know that you are beautiful, my intimate companion, know
that you are beautiful! Your eyes are doves behind your veil,
your hair is like a flock of goats that leap down from Mount
Gilead. 2Your teeth are like a flock of sheep shorn clean, that
have come up from their washing; all of them bearing twins,
and there is not one among them bereaved of her young.
3Your lips are like a scarlet thread, and your voice is lovely.
Like halves of a pomegranate are your cheeks behind your
veil. 4Your throat is like the tower of David, built with
courses of stones; a thousand shields are hung upon it, all
the quivers of the mighty men. 5Your two breasts are like
two fawns, twins of a gazelle that grazed among the lilies.

6"Until the day begins, and the shadows flee, I will myself go to
the mountain of myrrh and to the hill of frankincense.

7"Every part of you is beautiful, my intimate companion, and
there is no blemish in you. 8Come with me from Lebanon,
my bride, come with me from Lebanon! Travel with me

from the mountaintop of Amana, from the mountaintop of
Senir, from the mountaintop of Herman, from the dwelling
places of lions and the hill-country of leopards.

9“You have seduced me, my sister, my bride, you have seduced
me with one glance from your eyes, with one pearl of your
necklace. 10How attractive are your sexual intimacies, my
sister, my bride! How pleasing are your erotic moves, more
than wine; and the fragrance of your lotions is more pleasing
than all the spices. 11Your lips drip flowing honey, my bride;
honey and milk are under your tongue, and the fragrance of
your clothing is like the fragrance of Lebanon.

12“You are a garden that is locked, my sister, my bride, a
fountain that is locked, a spring that is sealed. 13Your
branches are a forest of pomegranates with choice fruit,
henna, and nard plants, 14nard and saffron, cane and
cinnamon, with all the trees of frankincense, myrrh, and
aloes, including the best spices. 15You are spring for the
gardens, a well of living waters, and streams flowing from
Lebanon.”

The Shulammite

16“Awaken, O north wind; and come, O south wind. Make the
scent of my garden waft out. Let its perfume be poured out.
May my lover come to his garden and eat its choice fruits.”

Song of Songs Chapter Five (Verse 1)

Solomon

1“I have come to my garden, my sister, my bride; I have plucked
my myrrh with my spice. I have eaten my honeycomb with
my honey; I have drunk my wine with my milk.”

Daughters of Jerusalem

“Eat, lovers! Drink and be drunk on sexual intimacies.”

Commentary

Husbands, I need to give you some advice before we go any further: Don't quote the compliments of this chapter directly to your wives. These compliments worked in ancient Israel, but they don't translate well into our culture.

When Solomon tells his bride her hair is like goats leaping down Mount Gilead, we don't swoon. When he says her teeth are like freshly-washed sheep, we are left puzzled; and as I wrote previously, when he compares her to a horse, we're offended.

But here's what you need to understand: In that culture, at that time, these were profound compliments. Solomon was saying, "You are beautiful in every way." He was noticing her, affirming her, speaking life to her. The specific metaphors might not work for us, but the principle absolutely does.

Every husband should be affirming his wife. Every wife should be affirming her husband. Every believer should understand that Jesus is constantly affirming us, noticing us, speaking words of life over us.

The Language of Love

"Know that you are beautiful, my intimate companion, know that you are beautiful. Your eyes are doves behind your veil. Your hair is like a flock of goats that leap down from Mount Gilead. Your teeth are like a flock of sheep shorn clean that have come up from their washing, all of them bearing twins, and there is not one among them bereaved of her young. Your lips are like a scarlet thread and your voice is lovely. Like halves of a pomegranate are your cheeks behind your veil." (4:1-3)

Solomon is going through his bride's features one by one, affirming each one. He says "beautiful" twice in the first sentences—he wants her to *know* it, to really believe it.

"Your eyes are doves." We've seen this before. Doves are peaceful, gentle, pure. It's a compliment we can understand.

"Your hair is like goats leaping down Mount Gilead." This means flowing, cascading, moving like a herd of dark goats bounding down a mountainside. It's poetic. It's about movement and life, not about looking like an actual goat.

"Your teeth are like freshly-washed sheep." This one requires a bit more explanation. When sheep are first sheared and then washed, they are pristine white. She has all her teeth—"all of them bearing twins," meaning they are paired up, none missing. In a time before modern dentistry, this was significant. He's saying, "When you smile, it dazzles me because your teeth are so white and you haven't lost any."

We might say, "I love your smile." He says, "Your teeth are like washed sheep." Same idea, different ways of saying it.

"Your lips are like a scarlet thread." Red lips. Healthy complexion.

"Your voice is lovely." He likes hearing her speak.

"Your cheeks are like pomegranate halves." Pinkish-red, healthy, beautiful.

He is being thoroughly complimentary, going through feature after feature, letting her know he notices her, he appreciates her, he finds her beautiful.

Now, here's where this becomes important for us: *This is how Jesus sees us.*

Jesus the Encourager

We don't know exactly what Jesus looks like physically—though if he has appeared to you, you might have some idea. But we know his character. We know how he speaks to us.

Jesus is the Encourager-in-Chief. The Holy Spirit is called the Helper (Paraclete), but that word also means Encourager. One of God's primary activities in our lives is encouragement.

Why? Because the world beats us down constantly. Satan accuses us relentlessly. We face criticism, rejection, failure, disappointment. We get marked by this world. We accumulate scars, wounds, and insecurities.

Jesus sees all of it. He knows every imperfection, every failure, every scar. But he still says, "You are beautiful. You are lovely. You are mine."

He doesn't ignore our flaws. He's not pretending we're perfect. But he is working with us, covering us with his grace, progressively transforming us. While he is doing that work, he is constantly encouraging us. "I see you. I know you. You're beautiful to me."

The Importance of the Picture Hidden in Human Relationships

The Apostle Paul understood how important this understanding of human sexuality is. In 1 Timothy 4:1-3, he warned about false teachers who would forbid marriage and advocate abstaining from foods. These teachings come from demons, he said, and through hypocritical liars whose consciences are seared.

Some in church history have treated sex—even within marriage—as inherently sinful. Augustine and many like him felt there was no way anyone could be involved in sexual activity without some taint of sin. Therefore, they reasoned, church leaders shouldn't be involved in something so evil and should remain celibate.

But that's a misunderstanding of what God created. He designed it for marriage. Though the devil and the world do all they can to corrupt and degrade eros, the Lord celebrates it in the Song of Songs. It's not evil. It's not tainted. It's good, and it's meant to be enjoyed within the covenant of marriage. It is intended to reflect Christ and his church. Solomon's relationship with his bride helps us see Jesus' relationship with us.

When Jesus affirms us, when he speaks words of life over us, when he notices our beauty despite our imperfections—he is doing what Solomon does here. He's being the ultimate Encourager.

Teeth and Relationships

Let me give you a detail that might seem strange but is actually quite profound. In prophetic circles, teeth often represent relationships.

Why? Because of these verses in Song of Songs. When God shows someone a picture of teeth in a dream or vision, it's usually about relationships—because that's how teeth function here. Solomon is talking about the relationship between him and his bride, and he mentions her teeth as part of his affirmation of her.

Relationships are essential in the body of Christ. We're meant to be connected, to function together, to support one another. God cares deeply about how we handle our relationships.

Remember the Lord's Prayer: "Forgive us our debts as we forgive our debtors." Our relationship with God is connected to our forgiveness of others. Why? Because relationship matters that much to God.

Human beings have a hardness in them that can hold grudges and destroy relationships. That's not God's intent. *"If you are able, as far as it depends on you, live in peace with all men" (Romans 12:18).* The apostle Peter speaks clearly how we are to treat the day-to-day sins of those around us, *"Love conceals a great number of sins" (1 Peter 4:8).*

Most of the offenses people commit against us, we can just forgive and move on. Someone steps on your toe walking through a crowd—love covers that. No big deal. It's just part of being human around other humans.

But when someone intentionally kicks you in the shins with malice aforethought, you probably need to address that. You say, "Please don't do that anymore." Even then, you release them in your heart. You forgive. You do everything you can to preserve the relationship as far as it's up to you.

Teeth represent relationship. And Solomon, when he looks at his bride, affirms the relationships. He says, "You're bearing twins. You haven't lost any. You're maintaining the connections I've called you to maintain." Jesus says the same thing to us.

Adding to Her Beauty

"Your throat is like the Tower of David, built with courses of stones. A thousand shields are hung upon it, all the quivers of the mighty men. Your two breasts are like two fawns, twins of a gazelle that grazed upon the lilies." (4:4-5)

Again, we're in imagery that doesn't quite translate. A throat like the Tower of David? What does that even mean?

The Tower of David was obviously well-regarded, well-built, imposing. It had places to hang weaponry. It was a place of strength and beauty. Solomon is probably referring to all the jewelry his bride wears around her neck—the necklaces, the pearls, the ornaments. He's saying, "Your neck is stately, and it displays all this adornment beautifully." And he continues appreciating every aspect of her.

There is one more thing that Solomon is doing with this allusion to the tower of David; he is foreshadowing the transformation of his bride. She is beginning to reflect a warrior's nature. She is transforming into a bride who is able to stand next to her warrior husband without embarrassment or timidity. She is beginning to become the one she is destined to be.

"Until the day begins and the shadows flee, I myself will go to the mountains of Myrrh and to the hill of frankincense." (4:6)

Here we have myrrh and frankincense together again. We saw them before in the victory procession from the wilderness. Now they appear in this sensual context of a husband exploring even the most intimate parts of his wife's body. And make no mistake, this is extremely explicit imagery. The mountains of myrrh, plural, are a clear reference to the Shulammite's breasts (see the same imagery used in Song 2:16). The hill of frankincense is a less-than-veiled reference to the Shulammite's vulva, which Solomon will clearly make reference to in Song 7:2.

But do not let the embarrassingly explicit language and imagery distract our attention from the spices that were in view. Myrrh and frankincense were brought to Jesus by the Magi—gold, frankincense, and myrrh. These are expensive, precious substances. They bookend Jesus' earthly life: myrrh at his birth, myrrh at his death (it was mixed with gall and offered to him on the cross).

This is veiled imagery about Christ, but as Christians knowing the full story, we can't miss the hints. This isn't just about Solomon and his intimacy with his bride. It's about Christ and his Church. The fragrances that welcomed Jesus into the world, that marked his death, that signify his presence—they are here in this love poem written a thousand years before he was born.

God was planning this all along. He was weaving hints and foreshadows throughout Scripture so that when Jesus came, those with eyes to see would recognize him.

No Blemish in You

"Every part of you is beautiful, my intimate companion, and there is no blemish in you." (4:7)

There it is. The statement that echoes through into the New Testament.

Solomon says to his bride, "There is no blemish in you."

Paul writes in Ephesians 5:25-27: "*Husbands, sacrificially love your wives, just as also Christ sacrificially loved the Church and gave himself on her behalf in order that he might purify her, having cleansed her with the washing of water by the word, in order that he might present her to himself a magnificent Church, having no stain or wrinkle or any other such thing, but that she be holy and blameless.*"

No blemish. No stain. No wrinkle. Holy and blameless.

That's what Jesus is working toward. That's the bride he is preparing. Even while he is working on us, even while we're in process, he looks at us and says, "You're beautiful. You're mine. I'm going to present you to me without blemish."

This should blow our minds. We know our blemishes. We see our stains. We're aware of our wrinkles and imperfections. We look in the mirror and think, "How could Jesus love me?"

But he does. More than that, he is committed to transforming us into the bride who truly has no blemish—not because we earned it or achieved it, but because he cleansed us, purified us, washed us, and is progressively sanctifying us until we stand before him perfect.

The Invitation to Come

"Come with me from Lebanon, my bride. Come with me from Lebanon. Travel with me from the mountaintop of Amman, from the mountaintop of Senir, from the mountaintop of Hermon, from the dwelling places of lions and the hill country of leopards." (4:8)

Solomon is inviting his bride to leave her homeland in northern Israel—the Lebanon region with its mountains and dangers—and come be with him. He's saying, "I want you with me all the time, not just on occasional visits."

Remember, Solomon has many wives. He doesn't *need* her to visit more often. But he *wants* her with him. He's infatuated. He's captured by her.

"You have seduced me, my sister, my bride. You have seduced me with one glance from your eyes, with one pearl of your necklace." (4:9)

He is saying, "You've overwhelmed me. You've captured my heart. Just one look from you, and I'm yours."

This is Jesus speaking to his Church. "You've captured my heart. Come be with me. I want you with me all the time."

Here's where the test of inconvenience (which we will see fully in the next chapter) begins to reveal itself. Because sometimes Jesus calls us at inconvenient times. Sometimes he wants to spend time with us in the middle of the night, or when we're busy, or when we'd rather be doing something else.

Will we respond? Or will we say, "Not now, Lord. I'm comfortable. I'm in bed. It's inconvenient."

Solomon is saying to his bride, "I want you with me." She's going to have to decide: Is she willing to make that level of commitment? Is she willing to be inconvenienced for the sake of the relationship?

We will see her answer soon enough.

The Beauty of Intimacy

"How attractive are your sexual intimacies, my sister, my bride! How pleasing are your erotic moves, more than wine; and the fragrance of your lotions is more pleasing than all the spices. Your lips drip flowing honey, my bride, honey and milk are under your tongue, and the fragrance of your clothing is like the fragrance of Lebanon." (4:10-11)

Solomon is thoroughly delighted with his bride. Everything about her—her love, her physical responses to their sexual activities, her presence—it all enthralls him. The atmosphere she creates, the fragrances she wears, the way she speaks, the way she loves—all of it brings him joy.

This is the dynamic God wants with us. He wants to be thoroughly delighted in us. He wants to receive our worship, our service, our obedience as a pleasing fragrance.

We looked at this passage in Second Corinthians in the first chapter. But it is worth reviewing in this context. Second Corinthians 2:14-15 says, "*But thanks be to God, who always reveals who we are in Christ, and makes the fragrance of the knowledge of Christ known through us in every place. For we are the fragrance of Christ to God among those who are being saved, and among those who are perishing.*"

We're a fragrance to God. The things we do in obedience to him, the way we serve him, the way we worship him—it all rises to him like a pleasing aroma.

Solomon is saying to his bride, "Everything about you pleases me." Jesus is saying to his Church, "Everything you do for me in love and obedience—it delights me. I receive it. I'm pleased by it."

We have the ability to bring God joy. Let that sink in. The Creator of the universe, the Sovereign Lord, the King of Kings—he can experience joy because of what we do. Our worship matters to him. Our obedience pleases him. Our love for him brings him delight.

That's staggering. It should motivate us to live in a way that brings him joy.

The Locked Garden

"You are a garden that is locked, my sister, my bride, a fountain that is locked, a spring that is sealed." (4:12)

She's faithful. That's what this means. She's a locked garden—she's kept herself for him alone. As far as anyone else is concerned, they have no access. But for Solomon, she'll open the door and experience sexual intimacy with him.

It is vital that we understand this: God is jealous for us. Second Corinthians 11:2 says, *"For I am jealous for you with a godly jealousy, for I promised you in marriage to one husband, to present you as a pure virgin to Christ."*

God doesn't want us being promiscuous with the world. He doesn't want us opening ourselves to every influence, every temptation, every distraction. He wants us to be a locked garden—faithful to him, set apart for him, kept for him alone.

But for him, we unlock the door. We open ourselves fully. We invite him in. We give him complete access to every part of our lives.

That's what it means to be a locked garden. Not that we're closed off and unavailable, but that we're reserved for our Beloved. We're his alone.

The Picture of Living Water

"Your branches are a forest of pomegranates with choice fruit, henna and nard plants, nard and saffron, cane and cinnamon, with all the trees of frankincense, myrrh, and aloes, including the best spices. You are a spring

for the gardens, a well of living water, and streams flowing from Lebanon." (4:13-15)

All this imagery about forests and spices—it's beautiful poetry, but it's hard for us to fully grasp without living in that agricultural context.

But then we get to something that clicks: "You are a spring for the gardens, a well of living water."

Living water. Where have we heard that before?

Jesus said in John 7:38-39, "*The one who believes in me, just as the Scripture states, rivers of living water will flow from his midsection. But he said this in reference to the Spirit whom those who believed in Jesus were about to receive, for the Spirit was not yet given because Jesus was not yet glorified.*"

Living water flows from the bride of Christ. The Holy Spirit dwelling in us flows out to touch others. We become sources of life in a dying world.

Solomon is saying to his bride, "You provide life. You're not just beautiful to me—you're life-giving. You're a source of refreshment and blessing."

But here's where I think the poetry shifts. How could Solomon's bride be a spring of living water to the gardens? In the literal, physical relationship, that's hard to picture.

But in the relationship between Christ and the Church? That makes perfect sense. We *are* living water to the world. Jesus dwelling in us by his Spirit flows out through us to bring life to others.

I think at this point in the Song, the Holy Spirit is emphasizing the Christ-and-Church interpretation more than the Solomon-and-bride interpretation. The poetry is becoming more obviously about Jesus and his people than about a human marriage.

Both layers are present throughout the book, but sometimes one is more prominent than the other.

The Bride's Response

"Awaken, O north wind; and come, O south wind. Make the scent of my garden waft out. Let its perfume be poured out. May my lover come to his garden and eat its choice fruits." (4:16)

Finally, the bride speaks. And her response is beautiful.

She wants her fragrance to go out into the world. She wants the atmosphere she's creating with her beloved to spread beyond their private place. She wants everyone to know—this relationship is real, it's powerful, it's beautiful.

But notice her focus: "May my lover come to his garden."

She's not doing this for the world's sake. She's doing it to draw her husband. Yes, the world will benefit. Yes, others will notice. But her primary motivation is him.

It is critical that we understand this. We don't serve the world for the world's sake. We serve the world for Jesus' sake. We reach out to others because it brings him glory, because it draws his attention, because it pleases him.

Sometimes we get so caught up in ministry, in reaching people, in making a difference, that we forget the primary relationship. We start serving the world and neglecting the One we're supposed to be serving.

The bride keeps her focus right: "I want the fragrance to go out so that my lover will be drawn to me."

We should want the same thing. Our prayer is, "Lord, let our ministry, our service, our witness draw your attention. Let it bring you glory. Let it please you. Yes, let it bless others—but ultimately, we're doing this for you."

Solomon's Response

"I have come to my garden, my sister, my bride. I have plucked my myrrh with my spice. I have eaten my honeycomb with my honey. I have drunk my wine with my milk." (5:1a)

He responds to her invitation. She called, and he came. She unlocked the garden, and he entered. This is intimate language. This is a husband and wife together, enjoying each other fully.

It is also a picture of Jesus responding when his bride invites him. When we open ourselves to him, when we make ourselves available, when we prioritize the relationship—he comes. He responds. He enters in.

The Chorus Responds

"Eat, lovers, drink and be drunk on sexual intimacies." (5:1b)

The daughters of Jerusalem, the chorus observing this relationship, respond with celebration. They are not embarrassed. They are not offended. They say, "Yes! This is beautiful! Enjoy each other fully!"

This is the body of Christ at its best. When we see someone stepping into deeper intimacy with Jesus, we celebrate. We don't get jealous or critical. We say, "Yes! That's what we want! That's what this is all about!"

We praise each other's intimate love for Jesus. We encourage each other to go deeper. We celebrate when someone experiences breakthrough, when God touches someone powerfully, when a brother or sister steps into new levels of relationship with him.

That's what the daughters of Jerusalem represent—the community of faith that affirms and celebrates intimate relationship with God.

The Principle for Marriage

Before we close this chapter, let me bring it back to human relationships for a moment.

Husbands and wives: Are you affirming each other? Are you speaking life over one another? Are you noticing the beauty in your spouse and saying so? Or have you fallen into the trap of taking each other for granted, of only pointing out flaws, of letting criticism replace affirmation?

Solomon models something important here. He goes through his bride's features one by one, finding something beautiful to say about each one. He's generous with his compliments. He makes her feel seen, noticed, appreciated.

Every husband should do this. Not with the exact metaphors Solomon uses—please, don't tell your wife her hair looks like goats. But with genuine, specific, generous affirmation. "I love your smile." "You look beautiful today." "I appreciate how you…" "I noticed that you…" "You're amazing at…" Speak life. Affirm. Encourage.

Wives, do the same for your husbands. The Shulammite isn't passive in this relationship. She responds with her own affirmations, her own expressions of love and appreciation.

This is how marriages stay "fresh and green." Not by accident, but by intentional, consistent affirmation and appreciation.

It is how our relationship with Jesus stays fresh and green too. We tell him we love him. We thank him for specific things. We worship him. We express our affection and appreciation. He is doing it constantly for us—affirming, encouraging, speaking life. We should do the same back to him.

In our marriages, we should reflect that same dynamic—constant affirmation, generous encouragement, consistent expressions of love.

That's what this chapter is about. Words matter. Affirmation matters. Encouragement matters. Solomon knew it. Jesus demonstrates it constantly.

Now it's our turn to live it.

6
THE BUMP IN THE ROAD

Chapter Five (Verses 2-16)

The Shulammite

2“I was asleep, but my heart was awake. A sound, my lover is knocking!”

Solomon

“Open to me, my sister, my intimate companion, my dove, my perfect one; for my head is covered with dew, my strands of hair with the moisture of the night.”

The Shulammite

3“I have taken off my gown, how can I possibly put it on? I have washed my feet, how can I soil them?

4“My lover put his hand to the opening, and my intimate parts were aroused for him. 5I got ready to open for my lover. My hand dripped with myrrh, and my fingers with flowing myrrh on the handles of the lock. 6I opened for my lover, but my lover had turned away, he had gone his way. My soul went out as he turned his back. I tried to search for him but did not find him. I called him, but he did not answer.

7"Those who keep watch doing their rounds in the city found me. They struck and bruised me. They took my veil away from me, the ones who watch the walls.

8"I earnestly urge you all, daughters of Jerusalem, if you find my lover, this is what you should say to him: I am faint with love."

The Daughters of Jerusalem

9"What is your lover more than another lover, O loveliest of women? What is your lover more than another lover that you so earnestly entreat us?"

The Shulammite

10"My lover is radiant and red, prominent among ten thousand.
11His head is like gold that is refined; his strands of hair are
waving palm branches, black as a raven. 12His eyes are like
doves upon streams of waters, bathed in milk, dwelling
beside a pool. 13His cheeks are like garden beds of spice,
terraces of fragrant spice; his lips are lilies dripping with
flowing myrrh. 14His hands are rods of gold set with topaz;
his genitals are polished ivory trimmed with sapphires. 15His
thighs are columns of alabaster established on bases of
refined gold; his physique is like Lebanon, chosen like the
cedars. 16His mouth is sweet, and he is entirely desirable.
This is my lover, this is my companion, O daughters of
Jerusalem."

Song of Songs Chapter Six (Verses 1-3)

The Daughters of Jerusalem

1"Where has your lover gone, O loveliest of women? Where has your lover turned, so that we might seek him with you?"

The Shulammite

[2]"My lover has gone to his garden, to the garden beds of spice,
to graze in the gardens and to gather lilies. [3]I am my lover's,
and my lover is mine. He grazes among the lilies."

Commentary

Everything has been building beautifully. The love is fresh, the affirmations are flowing, the intimacy is deepening. Solomon and the Shulammite are clearly enamored with each other. The relationship seems perfect.

And then it happens.

The bump in the road. The mistake. The moment that changes everything.

The Knock at the Door

"I was asleep but my heart was awake. A sound—my lover is knocking. 'Open to me, my sister, my intimate companion, my dove, my perfect one, for my head is covered with dew, my strands of hair with the moisture of the night.'" (5:2)

This is a new scene, a new poem. The Shulammite is in bed. It's late—we know because the dew has already fallen. She's not in deep sleep, but she's drowsy, comfortable, settled in for the night.

Then she hears it: knocking. Solomon's voice. He's calling to her. He wants to be with her and enjoy sexual intimacy with her.

Notice his words: "Open to me." He's not demanding. He's not forcing his way in. He's asking. He's inviting. He's giving her the choice.

"My sister, my intimate companion, my dove, my perfect one." He's affirming her even as he asks. He's reminding her of who she is to him and of their intimate physical relationship.

"My head is covered with dew, my strands of hair with the moisture of the night." He's been out late. He's come to her despite the hour, despite the inconvenience. He wants to be with her.

This is Jesus knocking at the door of his Church.

Revelation 3:20: "*Look, I have taken a stand at the entrance and I am knocking. If anyone hears my voice and opens the door, I will come into him and I will dine with him and he with me.*"

Jesus stands at the door. The tense in Greek (the perfect tense) means he has taken his stand and remains there. That's where he is. That's where he stays. Knocking. Waiting. Calling.

Will we open the door?

The Ancient Equivalent of "Not Tonight, Dear"

"I have taken off my gown, how can I possibly put it on? I have washed my feet. How can I soil them?" (5:3)

Oh no.

She says, "No."

She doesn't say it directly. She doesn't say, "Go away." But she makes excuses. She lists reasons why it is inconvenient. She's already undressed for bed. She's already washed her feet (which, in that culture, you did before getting into bed). If she gets up now, she'll have to do it all over again.

It's too much trouble. It's inconvenient. She's comfortable where she is.

This is the test of inconvenience.

And she fails.

We need to understand how serious this is. This isn't just any man knocking. This is Solomon—the king, her husband, the one who has showered her with love and affirmation and gifts. He has plenty of other places he could go. He has other wives, other opportunities with his many concubines, but he has chosen to come to her door.

And she says, "No."

When we transpose this to Christ and the Church, the severity becomes even more clear. Jesus—the King of Kings, the Lord of Lords, the One who died for us—is knocking at our door. He wants to spend time with us. He wants intimacy with us.

We say, "Not now, Lord. I'm comfortable. I'm in bed. It's inconvenient."

How many times have we done this? He wakes us in the night with a dream or a word, and we roll over and go back to sleep. He calls us to prayer, and we say, "Later—I'm busy right now." He invites us to worship, and we check our phones instead. He prompts us to reach out to someone, and we ignore the nudge because it is uncomfortable.

He knocks, and we make excuses.

This is the church in Laodicea. The lukewarm church. The church that has everything it needs materially but has locked Jesus outside. He's standing at the door of his own church, knocking, asking to be let in.

Solomon's Response

"My lover put his hand to the opening, and my intimate parts were aroused for him." (5:4)

The imagery of the opening is deliberately vague in Hebrew. Some translations try to make it specific—"He put his hand through the latch" or something like that. But the literal text is more ambiguous: "My lover put his hand to the opening."

I think this vagueness is intentional because this is more about Christ and the Church than about Solomon and the Shulammite at this particular moment. Jesus reaches through to touch his bride's spirit. He creates longing in her heart even though she's refused him.

However, this metaphor is built on the reality of a sexual relationship between a husband and wife. So when Solomon reaches to touch his bride, her body responds."My intimate parts were aroused for him."

This is explicit language intended for a mature audience. Suddenly, she realizes what she's done. Suddenly, she wants him. Desire is awakened—not by her own choice, but by his touch. His touch creates the desire in her body that her mind had not yet felt.

God does this. When we refuse him, when we're too comfortable or too busy or too distracted, he sometimes reaches in and touches our hearts. He creates desire. He reminds us of what we're missing.

We wake up—spiritually, emotionally—and then think, "What am I doing? Why did I refuse him?"

Too Late

"I got ready to open for my lover. My hand dripped with myrrh, and my finger with flowing myrrh on the handles of the door lock. I opened for my lover, but my lover had turned away. He had gone his way. My soul went out as he turned his back. I tried to search for him, but did not find him. I called him, but he did not answer." (5:5-6)

She moves quickly to open herself to her lover. But he is gone.

She had her chance, and she missed it. Solomon waited, but not forever. When she didn't respond, he left. He had other places to go.

Now she's desperate. "*My soul went out as he turned his back.*" She's devastated. She realizes what she's lost.

She goes out searching. She calls for him. But there's no answer.

This is what happens when we refuse Jesus' invitation. We lose the immediacy of his presence. We enter a season of distance, of apparent absence, of searching without finding.

It's not that he has abandoned us. It's not that he has stopped loving us. But he is teaching us a lesson: "You can't take my presence for granted. You can't assume I'll always be available on your terms. When I knock, you need to answer."

The Watchmen Again

"Those who keep watch doing their rounds in the city found me. They struck and bruised me. They took my veil away from me, the ones who watched the walls." (5:7)

Remember the watchmen from Chapter 3? When the Shulammite went out searching for Solomon the first time, during the test of absence, the watchmen let her pass. They gave her grace.

Not this time.

This time, they treat her like a prostitute. They strike her. They bruise her. They take away her veil—the symbol of her modesty, her respectability. By removing her veil, they are publicly proclaiming, "This woman is a prostitute. This is what she is."

Why the different treatment? Because grace has been lifted. She's not just seeking her beloved during his absence. She's seeking him after she refused him. She's reaping the consequences of her choice.

The watchmen—representing the culture, the society, the world—they don't see a faithful wife searching for her husband. They see a woman out at night without her husband, and they draw the obvious (wrong) conclusion.

This is what happens to the church when we refuse Jesus. When we lock him outside, when we're content to have good meetings without the Holy Spirit, when we're comfortable with religion but not relationship—the world looks at us and says, "You're just in it for the money. You're hypocrites. You're no different from anyone else."

They are wrong, of course. But from their perspective, what else can they think? If we don't have the presence and power of God distinguishing us, if we look just like any other social club or nonprofit organization, why would they think we're anything special?

Jesus said, "*If salt loses its flavor, it is good for nothing except to be thrown out and trampled by men.*" That's exactly what's happening here. The bride has lost her distinctiveness, and now she's being trampled by the very people who should have respected her.

Calling for Help

"I earnestly urge you, all daughters of Jerusalem, if you find my lover, this is what you should say to him: I am faint with love." (5:8)

Now she's desperate enough to ask for help. She's calling out to the other women—the daughters of Jerusalem, the community of faith—and saying, "If you see him, tell him I'm faint with love. Tell him I need him."

She's starting to vocalize her need. She's admitting she made a mistake. She's acknowledging that she can't fix this on her own.

This is good. This is progress. When we've refused Jesus and entered a wilderness season, one of the critical steps is admitting we need him. Crying out to other believers. Asking for help. Saying, "I messed up. I need to find him again."

Pride keeps us isolated in our wilderness. Humility reaches out for help.

What Makes Your Lover Special?

"What is your lover more than another lover, O loveliest of women? What is your lover more than another lover that you so earnestly entreat us?" (5:9)

The daughters of Jerusalem ask a reasonable question: "What's so special about him? Why are you so desperate? What makes this relationship worth all this pain and searching?"

This is the question the world asks the Church: "Why is Jesus so important to you? What makes him different from any other religious figure? Why does this matter so much?"

We need to have an answer.

First Peter 3:15 says, *"Always be ready to offer an explanation to anyone who asks you about the reason you are filled with hope, doing so with kindness and respect."*

Can you explain why Jesus matters to you? Can you articulate what he has done in your life? Can you give a testimony that makes people understand why this relationship is worth everything?

The Shulammite is about to do exactly that.

Describing the Beloved

"My lover is radiant and red, prominent among ten thousand. His head is like gold that is refined. His strands of hair are waving palm branches, black as a raven. His eyes are like doves upon streams of water, bathed in milk, dwelling beside a pool. His cheeks are like garden beds of spice, terraces of fragrant spice. His lips are lilies dripping with flowing myrrh. His hands are rods of gold set with topaz. His genitals are polished ivory trimmed with sapphire. His thighs are columns of alabaster established on bases of refined gold. His physique is like Lebanon, chosen like the cedars. His mouth is sweet and he is entirely desirable. This is my lover. This is my companion, O daughters of Jerusalem." (5:10-16)

She goes through Solomon's features one by one, in embarrassing detail, just as he did for her earlier. She's evangelizing. She's explaining why he is worth pursuing. She's painting a picture of his beauty, his character, his virility, and his worthiness in an intimate and revealing way. Note how she graphically describes Solomon's sexual organs without embarrassment. She is unapologetically captivated by every part of him.

"He's prominent among ten thousand." He stands out. He's not just one option among many. He's the one.

All the imagery—gold, doves, spices, alabaster, cedar—it's poetic language to say, "He's perfect. He's wonderful. He's everything."

Then the summary: "He is entirely desirable. This is my lover. This is my companion."

This is what we should be able to say about Jesus. When someone asks why he matters, we should be able to describe his character, his love, his worthiness. We should be able to say, "Let me tell you about my Jesus."

Not just doctrinal facts, not just theological arguments, but personal testimony. This is who he is to me. This is what he has done. This is why I can't stop pursuing him even when I've failed him.

Where Has He Gone?

"Where is your lover gone, O loveliest of women? Where has your lover turned so that we might seek him with you?" (6:1)

The daughters of Jerusalem are moved by her description. They want to help. They are saying, "Okay, we get it. He's special. So where is he? Let's go find him together."

This is the body of Christ supporting each other. When someone is in a wilderness season, when they are trying to reconnect with Jesus after a time of distance, we don't judge them. We don't lecture them. We say, "Let's go find him together."

The Honest Answer

"My lover has gone to his garden, to the garden beds of spice, to graze in the gardens and to gather lilies. I am my lover's and my lover is mine. He grazes among the lilies." (6:2–3)

Her answer is brutally honest: "He's gone to his other gardens. He has other places to go. I'm not his only option."

This is Solomon, after all. He has many wives, many "gardens." When she refused him, he went elsewhere.

But notice the end of her answer: "I am my lover's and my lover is mine."

Despite everything, despite her failure, despite the fact that Solomon is spending time with one of his other wives or concubines, she still claims the relationship. She still believes they belong to each other. She's taking responsibility—she knows whose fault it is that he has gone—but she's not giving up on the relationship.[3]

For us, this is acknowledging that Jesus has many people. He's ministering to others while we are in our wilderness. He's touching lives, answering prayers, building his kingdom through his many servants. He doesn't stop working just because we're not responding to him.

But we're still his, and he is still ours. The relationship hasn't ended. It's just not what it was. Restoration is possible if we keep pursuing.

The Cost of Refusal

Let's be clear about what happened here: The bride refused her husband when he came knocking, and there were consequences.

She lost immediate access to him.

She entered a season of searching without finding.

She faced public humiliation and mistreatment.

She had to humble herself and ask for help.

These aren't arbitrary punishments. These are natural consequences. When we refuse Jesus, when we're too comfortable or too busy to respond to his call, we lose the immediacy of his presence. We enter a wilderness season where he feels distant. We face the world's contempt when they see us as hypocrites claiming to know God but not demonstrating his power. We have to humble ourselves and admit we need help.

God allows these consequences because he loves us too much to let us stay comfortable in our refusal. He wants us to learn that his

---

[3] At this point, of course, the comparison with our "one man, one woman" marriage breaks down. When we experience a "bump in the road," our only option is to press into relationship and fix it. But this story is a prophetic picture of Christ and his bride (the Church), and the story of Solomon and the Shulammite reflect this reality.

presence is not something we can take for granted. He wants us to understand that when he knocks, we need to answer—regardless of the inconvenience.

This is a sobering message. It's not the feel-good, "Jesus loves you just as you are" message that we like to hear. It's the challenging, "Jesus loves you too much to leave you where you are" message that we need to hear.

Yes, Jesus loves us unconditionally. Yes, his grace covers all our sins. Yes, he will never leave us or forsake us.

But he also disciplines those he loves. He allows consequences to mature us. He lets us feel the pain of distance so we will learn not to create that distance again.

The bump in the road is painful. The wilderness season is difficult. The public humiliation is humbling.

But it's all designed to produce a mature bride—one who has learned never to refuse the Bridegroom when he knocks.

A Word to the Church

This chapter is a word to the Church in America, to the Church in the West, to any congregation or believer who has grown comfortable without God's manifest presence.

We've learned to have good meetings without the Holy Spirit. We've got excellent music, polished preaching, efficient programs, beautiful buildings. We can put on a Sunday morning service that entertains people, meets their social needs, maybe even teaches them some Bible facts.

But is Jesus in it? Is his presence manifest? Is his power demonstrated? Or have we locked him outside while we do church without him?

He is knocking. He's been knocking for a long time. And he is saying, "Let me in. Let me be part of this. Let my presence be the distinguishing factor in your gatherings."

Some churches have responded. Some have said, "Yes, Lord, we need you. Come in. Take over. We don't want just a good meeting—we want you."

But many haven't. Many are still comfortable with Jesus on the outside, with religion without relationship, with form without power.

And he is allowing consequences. He's allowing those churches to become like salt that has lost its saltiness—good for nothing except to be trampled by people. He's allowing the world to look at us and say, "You're hypocrites. You're no different from anyone else."

It doesn't have to be this way. The door can still be opened. Jesus is still standing there, still knocking, still offering relationship.

But we have to respond. We have to say, "Yes, Lord, even if it's inconvenient. Even if it means changing how we do things. Even if it means getting uncomfortable. Come in. We need you."

The bump in the road can be a turning point. The wilderness can lead to restoration. The consequences can produce maturity.

But only if we stop making excuses and open the door.

He is knocking.

Do you hear him?

7
THE MATURING BRIDE

Chapter Six (Verses 4-13)

Solomon

4"You are beautiful as Tirzah, my intimate companion, as lovely
as Jerusalem, awe-inspiring as troops arrayed by their
divisions. 5Let your eyes wander from me, for they
overpower me; your hair is like a flock of goats that have
leaped down from Gilead. 6Your teeth are like a flock of
ewes that have come down from their washing, all of them
bearing twins, and there is not one among them bereaved of
her young. 7Like halves of a pomegranate are your cheeks
behind your veil.

8"There are sixty queens, and eighty concubines, and virgins too
numerous to count; 9but my dove, my perfect one is first, she
is her mother's first daughter; she is pure to the one who
bore her. The daughters of Jerusalem saw her and
pronounced her blessed, the queens and concubines saw her,
and they praised her."

Daughters of Jerusalem, Queens, and Concubines

10"Who is this woman that looks out like the dawn, lovely as
the full moon, pure as the sun, as awe-inspiring as troops
arrayed by their divisions."

The Shulammite

11"I went down into the orchard among the nut trees to look at
the greenness of the valley, to see if the vine has flourished
and the pomegranates had blossomed. 12Before I knew it,
my soul directed me to the chariots of my noble people."

The Charioteers

13"Move back, move back, O Shulammite; move back, move
back and let us look upon you."

The Daughters of Jerusalem

"Why would you look upon the Shulammite, as at the Dance of the Two Armies?"

Song of Songs Chapter Seven (Verses 1-6)

Solomon

1"How attractive are your feet, visible in sandals, O noble's
daughter! The curves of your hips are like jewelry, the work
of a craftsman's hand. 2Your navel is a round drinking cup, it
does not lack spiced wine. Your mons pubis[4] is a mound of
wheat encircled by lilies. 3Your two breasts are like two
fawns, twins of a gazelle. 4Your neck is like a tower of ivory.
Your eyes are pools in Heshbon by the gates of Bath-
Rabbim. Your nose is like the tower of Lebanon facing
Damascus. 5Your head is upon you like Carmel, and the hair
of your head is like purple thread. The king is captured by
your locks of hair.

6"How attractive and how delightful you are, O love, with all
your pleasures.

Commentary

The relationship has been tested. The bride has made a mistake—a costly mistake. She refused her husband when he came knocking, and

[4] Alternately, "pubic mound," or "vulva."

she's spent time in the wilderness dealing with the consequences. She's been publicly humiliated, she's searched without finding, she's had to humble herself and ask for help.

But something is changing. Through the pain, through the wilderness, something is being forged in her. She's not the same person who said, "I'm comfortable in bed, don't bother me." She's maturing. She's learning. She's being transformed.

Now we're going to see what that maturity looks like.

Solomon Responds

"You are beautiful as Tirzah, my intimate companion, as lovely as Jerusalem, awe-inspiring as troops arrayed by their divisions. Let your eyes wander from me, for they overpower me. Your hair is like a flock of goats that have leapt down from Gilead. Your teeth are like a flock of ewes that have come down from their washing, all of them bearing twins, and there is not one among them bereaved of her young. Like halves of a pomegranate are your cheeks behind your veil." (6:4–7)

Solomon hears what his bride has been saying. He hears her describing him to the daughters of Jerusalem. He hears her saying, "I am faint with love for him." And he responds.

Most of this imagery we've seen before—he is repeating compliments he has given her earlier. But there's something new. He says that she is "awe-inspiring as troops arrayed by their divisions."

We're starting to see a warrior bride emerge. Someone who's not just beautiful in a passive, decorative way, but someone who has inherent power. Someone who, when she shows up, makes enemies think twice.

There's a reason armies display their troops in formation before battle. Sometimes just seeing the organized power of a well-trained army is enough to make the other side back down. No battle needed—just the demonstration of strength and readiness.

Solomon is saying his bride has that kind of power. She's becoming awe-inspiring. She's becoming someone with authority and strength, not just physical beauty.

This is the bride of Christ emerging in maturity. We're not just meant to be pretty and passive. We're meant to be powerful. We're meant to have the kind of authority that makes demons flee, the kind of presence that changes atmospheres, the kind of spiritual strength that impacts the world around us. The wilderness is producing something in the bride. The testing is having its intended effect.

She Stands Out

"There are sixty queens and eighty concubines and virgins too numerous to count, but my dove, my perfect one is first. She is her mother's first daughter, she is pure to the one who bore her. The daughters of Jerusalem saw her and pronounced her blessed, the queens and concubines saw her and they praised her." (6:8-9)

Now we're getting somewhere. Solomon makes it explicit, yes, he has many wives, sixty queens at this point, eighty concubines, countless virgins in the palace. But among all of them, the Shulammite is special.

She stands out. She's "first"—not necessarily in order, but in importance, in his affection, in her place in his heart.

Even the other queens and concubines recognize it. They see her and say, "She's blessed. There's something different about her."

This is Jesus loving his Church. Yes, he loves all people. Yes, he is drawing many to himself. Yes, there are millions and billions who trust in him. But there's something special about the mature bride—the ones who have pressed through, who have learned always to answer the door, who have allowed the wilderness to refine them rather than defeat them.

When the bride emerges from the wilderness mature and devoted, even those who don't fully understand the relationship recognize there's something special happening.

Who Is This?

"Who is this woman that looks out like the dawn, lovely as the full moon, pure as the sun, as awe-inspiring as the troops arrayed by their divisions?" (6:10)

Here it is—the first "Who is this?" question about the bride herself.

The daughters of Jerusalem, the queens, and concubines are asking because they are seeing something they haven't seen before. They are seeing a woman who's different, who's maturing, who's starting to reflect her husband's character in visible ways.

They say that she "looks out like the dawn"—she's bringing light into darkness. She's the beginning of a new day.

She is "lovely as the full moon"—the moon reflects the sun's light. She's reflecting her husband's glory. Just as the moon has no light of its own but shines by reflecting the sun, the bride has no power of her own but shines by reflecting the Son.

She is "pure as the sun"—she's becoming like him. She's taking on his character. She's being transformed into his image.

She is "awe-inspiring as troops arrayed by their divisions"—there's that military imagery again. She has power. She has authority. She's not someone to be trifled with.

This is biblical imagery of the Church. We're meant to reflect Christ's light to the world. We're meant to be pure, progressively sanctified, becoming more like him every day. We're meant to have spiritual authority—to be warriors in the kingdom, demolishing strongholds, taking ground for Christ.

The question "Who is this?" is starting to be answered. This is the maturing bride. This is someone who has been through the wilderness and come out stronger. This is someone who is starting to look like her Beloved.

But we're not done yet. There's more development to come.

Among the Chariots

"I went down into the orchard among the nut trees to look at the greenness of the valley, to see if the vine has flourished and the pomegranates had blossomed. Before I knew it, my soul directed me to the chariots of my noble people." (6:11-12)

The Shulammite is out enjoying creation—checking on the gardens, seeing how things are growing. Suddenly, without planning it, she finds herself among the chariots.

Chariots were the tanks of that era. They displayed the military might, the instruments of war. She, a woman, a bride, ends up in the middle of them.

This is the mature bride stepping into spiritual warfare. She's not necessarily seeking it, but she finds herself there. Because as you mature in Christ, as you start looking more like him, as you develop authority and power, you inevitably end up in places of warfare.

You end up wrestling with principalities and powers. You end up confronting demonic strongholds in your city. You end up standing for truth in places where darkness wants to reign. You end up among the chariots—in the battle, whether you planned to be there or not.

This is part of maturity. The bride doesn't just have a private relationship with her Beloved. She steps into his work in the world. She takes on his battles. She stands where he would stand and fights what he would fight.

The Shulammite Revealed

"Move back, move back, O Shulammite, move back, move back, and let us look upon you." (6:13a)

The charioteers—the warriors, the military men—see her among them and they are enamored. They want her to stay so they can watch her, admire her, gaze at her.

They call her by a name she hasn't been called before: the Shulammite.

This is the first time in the entire Song that she's identified by this name. We've been calling her the Shulammite because we knew from this verse that's who she is. But this is the reveal—this is when everyone else learns her identity.

What does Shulammite mean? It's the feminine form of Solomon's name. She now has his name. It's saying, "She looks like him. She reflects him. She's become like him."

Solomon is from the Hebrew word "shalom"—peace. He was the man of peace, the one who built the temple, the one whose reign was characterized by rest and prosperity.

The Shulammite is becoming like Solomon. She's taking on his character. She's reflecting his nature. She's the feminine version of who he is.

For us, this is profound. As we mature in Christ, we don't just have a relationship with him—we become like him. His character is formed in us. His peace—not the world's peace, but his supernatural, transcendent peace—becomes ours. We start looking like him to the point where people can identify us by his name.

This is what the Holy Spirit is working toward in every believer. Romans 8:29 says God predestined us "*to conform to the image of his Son.*" Galatians 4:19 says Paul was in labor "*until Christ is formed*" in those to whom he wrote.

The goal isn't just relationship. The goal is transformation. The goal is to look so much like Jesus that people see him when they see us.

The Shulammite has reached a level of maturity where the warriors—those engaged in battle, those who understand what spiritual warfare looks like—recognize who she is. She's the Shulammite. She's the feminine Solomon. She looks like the Prince of Peace.

The Daughters of Jerusalem Respond

"Why would you look upon the Shulammite as at the Dance Of The Two Armies?" (6:13b)

The daughters of Jerusalem step in with a rebuke. They are saying to the charioteers, "Why are you staring at her like she's entertainment? She's not here for your amusement. She's the king's bride. Look to the king himself, not to his reflection."

This is extremely important. As Christians, when we see someone walking in power and authority, when we see someone who looks like Jesus, our temptation is to focus on that person. We want to follow them, learn from them, be near them.

But the mature response is to say, "Don't look at them—look at Jesus. They are just reflecting him. Go to the source."

We can learn from mature believers. We can be inspired by them. We can follow their example as they follow Christ. But we don't worship them. We don't make them our focus. We look past them to Jesus himself.

The daughters of Jerusalem understand this. They are saying, "She's special, yes. But she's special because of him. Look at him, not at her."

The Dance of the Two Armies?

Nobody knows for sure what this dance was. It might have been an actual dance. It might have been a famous battle. It might have been a play or performance. The phrase appears only here in Scripture, so we don't have other references to figure it out.

But the point is clear regardless: The charioteers are treating the Shulammite's presence as spectacle or entertainment, and the daughters of Jerusalem are saying, "That's not appropriate. She's not here to be watched like a performer. She's the king's bride, and she's reflecting the king. Turn your attention to him."

This is what mature believers should do for each other—redirect attention from ourselves to Jesus. When someone compliments our ministry, our teaching, our worship leading, our whatever—we say, "Thank you, but it's not me. It's him. Look at Jesus."

Paul said it in 1 Corinthians 4:7: "*What do you have that you did not receive? If you also received it, why are you boasting like you did not receive it?*"

Everything good in us is Jesus. Everything powerful is him working through us. Everything worth noticing is his character being formed in us.

So when people notice, we redirect. "Look at him."

Restoration Begins

"How attractive are your feet visible in sandals, oh noble's daughter. The curves of your hip are like jewelry, the work of a craftsman's hand. Your navel is a round drinking cup—it does not lack spiced wine. Your mons pubis is a mound of wheat encircled by lilies. Your two breasts are like two fawns, twins of a gazelle." (7:1-3)

Solomon is back, and he is making his intentions clear. He's seen her among the chariots. He's heard what the charioteers said about her. He's watched her mature and transform. And he is saying, "You're beautiful. All of you. Every part of you."

He starts with her feet, perhaps also reminded of the Dance of the Two Armies while she was among the chariots. Then he describes her body, appreciating every aspect.

This is intimate language. This is a husband who has been separated from his wife—not by his choice, but by hers—and now they are coming back together, and he desires her. In a previous reference to the Shulammite's body, he uses mountain imagery to speak of her breasts and her vulva. Here he drops all imagery and speaks of her beautiful feet, the attractive curves of her hips, her inviting navel, her enticing mons pubis (vulva), and her two youthful breasts. It is the transparent language of a husband who is fully enraptured by his wife.

Solomon is announcing, "I still want you. I'm still attracted to you. What happened before doesn't change how I feel about you."

Jesus does the same for us. When we've failed him, when we've refused him, when we've gone through a wilderness as a consequence —and then we come back, we mature, we learn our lesson—he doesn't hold it against us. He doesn't say, "Well, you blew it, so now you're second-tier in my kingdom."

He says, "You're still beautiful to me. You're still mine. Let's restore this relationship fully."

The Compliments Continue

"Your neck is like a tower of ivory. Your eyes are pools in Heshbon by the gates of Bath-Rabbim. Your nose is like the tower of Lebanon facing Damascus. Your head is upon you like Carmel, and the hair of your head is like purple thread. The king is captured by your locks of hair." (7:4-5)

Some of these don't translate well for us. A nose like a tower? That's not typically a compliment in our culture. But it's about stateliness. She is regal and impressive.

The point is that Solomon is thoroughly delighting in his bride. He's appreciating her completely. And he ends with, "The king is captured by your locks of hair."

She's captured him. He's enthralled. Despite everything, despite the refusal and the wilderness and the separation, he is still completely in love with her.

Full Appreciation

"How attractive and how delightful you are, O love, with all your pleasures." (7:6)

This is the summary statement: "Everything about you delights me." This is Jesus speaking to his Church, to his bride. When we're maturing, when we're becoming more like him, when we're reflecting his character—he is delighted. Everything we do in obedience to him, everything we offer to him in worship and service—it brings him pleasure. We're not trying to earn his love. We have that already. But we can bring him joy. We can delight him. We can please him.

That should motivate us. Not fear of punishment or trying to earn salvation. But the simple desire to please him who loves us so much.

Solomon is saying to his bride, "You delight me completely." Jesus is saying to us, "You delight me. Keep becoming who I'm making you to be. Keep maturing. Keep reflecting my character. It brings me joy."

The Identity Solidified

The Shulammite has come a long way. She started as an insecure young woman worried about her dark complexion, about not being beautiful enough, about being marked by the world.

Now she's someone the warriors recognize and admire. Someone the daughters of Jerusalem defend and celebrate. Someone who's been given a name that identifies her with the king himself—the Shulammite, the feminine Solomon.

She's become someone who reflects her husband's peace. Someone with authority and power. Someone who ends up in spiritual warfare without seeking it because that's where mature brides end up. Someone who has learned never to refuse the king when he knocks.

This is what maturity looks like. Not perfection—she's still growing, still learning. But there is progress, visible transformation, character development, and authority emerging.

This is who the Church is called to be. Not perfect, but maturing. Not without struggles, but learning from them. Not passive, but powerful. Not hiding from warfare, but stepping into it. Not just having a private relationship with Jesus, but reflecting him visibly enough that the world asks, "Who is this?"

We're not fully there yet. Neither was the Shulammite at this point in the Song. There's one more crucial development to come—the final revelation of who she is and what she does.

But we can see the trajectory. We can see where this is heading. The bride is maturing. The question "Who is this?" is starting to be answered.

8
SET ME AS A SEAL

Chapter Seven (Verses 7-13)

Solomon

7"Your stature is like a date palm tree, and your breasts are its
clusters. 8I said, 'I will climb the date palm. I will grasp the
dates.' Now may your breasts be like clusters of the vine, and
the breath of your nostrils like apricots. 9And may your
mouth be like the best wine."

The Shulammite

10"I am my lover's, and his sexual desire is focused on me.
11Come, my lover, let us go into the fields; let us spend the
night in the villages. 12Let us get up early and go to the
vineyards; let us see if the vine has budded, whether the
blossom has opened, whether the pomegranates are
flourishing. There I will make love with you. 13The
mandrakes have released their fragrance; and over our doors
are all precious gifts, new and old. I have kept them stored
away for you, my lover."

Song of Songs Chapter Eight (Verses 1-14)

The Shulammite

1"What if you were designated as a brother to me, an infant at the breasts of my mother? I would find you outside and I would kiss you, and they would not feel contempt for me. 2I would lead you, I would bring you to the house of my mother who taught me. I would give you spiced wine to drink from the sweet juice of my pomegranates.

3"His left hand is under my head, and his right hand caresses me.

4"I earnestly urge you all, daughters of Jerusalem, do not arouse, do not stir up sexual desire until love can take pleasure in it."

The Daughters of Jerusalem

5"Who is this coming up from the wilderness leaning against her lover?"

The Shulammite

"Under the apricot tree I aroused you; there your mother was pregnant with you, there she went into labor and gave birth to you.

6"Set me as a seal upon your heart, as a seal upon your arm, for sexual desire is as powerful as death, jealous passion is severe as Sheol. Its flames are flames of fire, the lightning of Yahweh.[5] 7Many waters are not able to extinguish love's sexual desire, nor rivers flood it; if a man gave all the wealth of his house for it, they would surely despise him."

Brothers of the Shulammite

8"We have a young sister, and she has no breasts. What should we do for our sister on the day when she is asked to marry?

---

[5] God's personal name (called the Tetragrammaton), Yahweh, is most often written as LORD in modern translations. It is also translated by some as Jehovah.

9If she is a wall, we will build defenses of silver; and if she is a door, we will secure her with planks of cedar."

The Shulammite

10"I was a wall, and my breasts became towers; then, in his eyes, I was as one who achieves peace.

11"A vineyard in Baal-Hamon belonged to Solomon; he gave the vineyard to those who care for vineyards. Each man was to bring a thousand silver coins for its fruit.

12"My vineyard is my own to share. The thousand silver coins are for you, O Solomon, and two hundred are for those who care for its fruit."

Solomon

13"You women who sit in the gardens, your husbands are listening attentively for your voice. Make your voices heard for me."

The Shulammite

14"Escape, my lover, and let yourself be like a gazelle or a youthful stag among the stags on the mountain of spices."

Commentary

We've nearly arrived at the climax of the Song. Everything has been building to this—this revelation of who the bride is and what she does. We are almost to the verse that came to me in a dream, repeating all night long until I woke up and knew I had to study it in depth.

This is the key that unlocks the entire book.

The Restoration Scene

First, before we get to that verse, we need to finish the restoration that began in the previous chapter. Solomon has been affirming his bride, expressing his continued desire for her. He now states his desire and purpose plainly:

"Your stature is like a date palm tree, and your breasts are its clusters. I said 'I will climb the date palm. I will grasp the dates.' Now may your breasts be like clusters of the vine, and the breath of your nostrils like apricots. And may your mouth be like the best wine." (7:7–9a)

Solomon is declaring his intent. This is reunion time. After the refusal, after the wilderness, after the separation—he is saying, "I want intimacy with you again." In expressive poetic language, he is expressing his desire to have intimacy with his wife.

The Shulammite responds immediately:

"May it flow smoothly to my lover, gliding over the lips of those who sleep together. I am my lover's, and his sexual desire is focused on me." (7:9b–10)

This time, she opens the door. This time, she doesn't make excuses. This time, she responds with enthusiasm, "I am my lover's, and his sexual desire is focused on me."

She's secure in the relationship. She knows she's his. She knows he wants her. She's not worried about the other queens and concubines. She's confident in her place in his heart.

This is the mature bride. Someone who has learned from her mistakes, someone who has been through the wilderness and come out stronger, someone who now responds immediately when her beloved calls.

The Invitation to Step into the World

"Come, my lover, let us go into the fields. Let us spend the night in the villages. Let us get up early and go to the vineyards. Let us see if the vine has budded, whether the blossom has opened, whether the pomegranates are flourishing. There I will make love with you. The mandrakes have released their fragrance, and over our doors are all precious gifts, new and old. I have kept them stored away for you, my lover." (7:11–13)

Now the bride is inviting her husband out into the world. She's saying, "Let's not just stay in the palace. Let's go out together. Let's experience the world together. Let's let the world see our relationship."

This is the Church saying to Jesus, "Let's go out into the world together. Let's minister together. Let's let people see our relationship, our love, our intimacy. Let's make your presence known everywhere we go."

The mandrakes releasing fragrance, the precious gifts both new and old—she's creating atmosphere, she's prepared gifts, she's saying, "Everything I have is for you. Everything I've stored up—all of it is yours."

This is the bride who has learned to give everything to her Beloved. She does not hold back. She does not keep things for herself. Everything is his.

The Wish for Public Affection

"What if you were designated as a brother to me, an infant at the breasts of my mother? I would find you outside and I would kiss you and they would not feel contempt for me. I would lead you. I would bring you to the house of my mother who taught me. I would give you spiced wine to drink from the sweet juice of my pomegranates." (8:1-2)

This is one of those things that doesn't quite translate into our culture. In that culture, public displays of affection between husband and wife were frowned upon. People didn't want to be reminded of the physical relationship. It was considered improper.

But brothers and sisters could show affection publicly—hugging, kissing on the cheek—and no one would think anything of it.

So the Shulammite is saying, "I wish I could show you affection in public without people judging me. I wish I could express my love for you anywhere, anytime, without having to hide it."

For us, this is saying we want to be able to express our love for Jesus openly, publicly, without shame or embarrassment. We want the world to see our affection for him. We want to be able to worship him, talk about him, demonstrate our relationship with him—anywhere, anytime. The mature bride isn't ashamed of her Beloved. She wants everyone to know about him.

The Intimate Moment

"His left hand is under my head and his right hand caresses me." (8:3)

This is the third time this exact phrase appears in the Song. It's an intimate moment—husband and wife lying together, close, connected, enjoying their sexual relationship.

Each time it appears, it's followed by the solemn warning.

The Warning—Third Time

"I earnestly urge you all, daughters of Jerusalem, do not arouse, do not stir up sexual desire until love can take pleasure in it." (8:4)

This is the third and final time this warning appears. By now, we understand it at a deeper level.

Yes, it's wise advice for physical relationships—don't awaken desires you're not ready to handle appropriately in marriage.

But it's also a warning about spiritual maturity. The Shulammite has learned this lesson the hard way. She awakened intimate desire before she was mature enough to handle it properly. She thought she was ready for the full relationship, but when it became inconvenient, she refused her husband.

Now, having been through the wilderness, having matured, having learned never to refuse him again—she issues the warning a third time. She's saying, "Learn from my mistake. Don't step into deep intimacy with the king until you're ready to respond to him always, regardless of convenience."

For us, this is about counting the cost of discipleship. Jesus said in Luke 14 that we need to sit down and calculate what it will cost to follow him. We need to be willing to give up everything if he asks. We need to be ready to take up our cross daily.

If we are pursuing deep experiences of God's presence, we need to be willing to develop the character and commitment that sustains us. We must be ready to answer the door whenever he knocks.

This is the third time this warning is spoken because it's of the utmost importance. It's a lesson the entire Song has been teaching. Maturity isn't just about having experiences—it's about being transformed into someone who always responds to the Beloved.

Who Is This? — The Final Answer

"Who is this coming up from the wilderness leaning against her lover?" (8:5a)

Here it is. The question Bobby Conner heard from the Lord. The central question of the entire Song.

Who is this?

This is different from the first "Who is this?" back in chapter three when they were asking about Solomon's sedan chair. This is different from the "Who is this?" in chapter six when they were asking about the Shulammite among the chariots.

This is the final revelation. This is the mature bride emerging from the wilderness.

Notice the key detail: She is *leaning against her lover.*

She is not walking apart from him. She is not standing on her own. She is not independent or self-sufficient. She is leaning, supported by him, dependent on him.

She's coming *up* from the wilderness—victorious, refined, transformed. But she's not coming alone or in her own strength. She's leaning on her Beloved every step of the way.

The daughters of Jerusalem notice the change. They see something different in her. They see someone who has been tested and has come through. Someone who is no longer self-reliant but is completely dependent on her husband.

This is the bride Jesus is seeking. Not someone who can do ministry in her own strength. Not someone who is impressive and independent. But someone who leans completely on him. Someone who knows she's absolutely dependent on him for everything.

We're the ones, the remnant, the bride, who need to lean into Jesus no matter what's going on around us. In the days we're living in, there will be plenty of opportunities to grow frightened and pull away. Many prophetic words tell us things are going to get intense. The world is going to shake.

But the mature bride doesn't lean away in fear. She leans *in* to Jesus. She presses closer. She becomes more dependent, not less.

Who is this coming up from the wilderness leaning on her lover?

This is the bride emerging in our generation. This is who we're called to be.

The Birthplace Remembered

"Under the apricot tree I aroused you. There your mother was pregnant with you. There she went into labor and gave birth to you." (8:5b)

The Shulammite gives a nod to the fact that the Jewish people birthed her husband. Solomon came from Israel, just as the Messiah came from the Jews.

For us as Christians, this is acknowledging that our spiritual heritage comes through the Jewish people. They stewarded the promises of God. They brought the Messiah into the world. Jesus came to them first.

Romans 11 tells us that we've been grafted into the olive tree. We don't replace Israel—we're added to the promise. And Paul says if we've received spiritual blessings from the Jews, we owe them support and prayer.

This isn't about politics. Israel as a modern nation is a political entity that can make good or bad decisions like any government. But the Jewish people as God's chosen people—they have promises that haven't been revoked. We owe them a debt of gratitude because they gave us our Savior.

The Shulammite acknowledges this. The bride remembers where her husband came from.

Set Me As a Seal

"Set me as a seal upon your heart, as a seal upon your arm, for sexual desire is as powerful as death. Jealous passion is severe as Sheol. Its flames are flames of fire, the lightning of Yahweh. Many waters are not able to extinguish love's desire, nor rivers flood it. If a man gave all the wealth of his house for it, they would surely despise him." (8:6-7)

This is the most powerful section of the entire book. This is where the mature bride declares her commitment and invites her husband's jealousy.

Let's break it down.

"Set me as a seal upon your heart, as a seal upon your arm."

A seal is permanent. Remember when Jesus was buried? They set a seal on the stone so it couldn't be opened. A seal means "lock this in place."

The bride is saying, "Put me on your heart permanently. Let me be sealed there so I can never be removed. Put me on your arm—your strength, your power, your authority—and seal me there."

She wants to be permanently attached to him. She's inviting him to be possessive, to claim her completely, to never let her go.

Then she describes what that jealousy looks like:

"Sexual desire is as powerful as death."

In that era, unless you were Enoch or Elijah, death had total power. No one escaped it. She's saying, "Let your desire for me be that powerful. Let it be as inevitable and inescapable as death."

"Jealous passion is severe as Sheol."

Sheol was the holding place of the dead. It's severe, it's serious, it's not something to trifle with. She's saying, "Let your jealousy for me be that intense."

"Its flames are flames of fire, the lightning of Yahweh."[6]

This is the only place in the entire Song where God's name appears. Some scholars want to translate it as just "mighty" or "powerful," which is a legitimate use of the word. But I believe God's personal name is intentionally here. This is divine fire, divine jealousy, divine passion.

The lightning was considered God's arrows. The Shulammite is saying, "Let the fire of your jealousy be God's fire. Let the lightning of your jealousy be God's arrows."

"Many waters are not able to extinguish love's desire, nor rivers flood it."

Fire and flood are the two great destructive forces. Isaiah 43:2 promises, "*When you cross over the waters, I am with you . . . When you walk through fire, you will not be singed.*"

She's saying, "Let this love be indestructible. Let it survive fire and flood. Let nothing be able to extinguish it."

"If a man gave all the wealth of his house for it, they would surely despise him."

True love can't be bought. You can hire a prostitute, but you can't purchase genuine love. If someone tries, people see through it and despise them for it.

Understanding the Jealousy

Now here's what the mature bride understands: She's inviting her husband to be intensely jealous for her. That means if she starts to wander, if she starts to be distracted by other things, if she begins to violate their relationship—he has permission to act.

---

[6] God's personal name (called the Tetragrammaton), Yahweh, is most often written as LORD in modern translations. It is also translated by some as Jehovah.

What does a jealous husband do when someone threatens his marriage? Proverbs tells us that a husband whose wife is being pursued by another man is dangerous. He's like fire in your lap. He can kill you, and it's considered a crime of passion—still murder, but with extenuating circumstances. A jealous husband protects what's his. He doesn't tolerate threats to the relationship.

The bride is saying, "I give you permission to be that jealous. I give you permission to act if I start to stray. I give you permission to do whatever it takes to keep me faithful to you."

This is profound for our relationship with Jesus.

God's Jealousy

The Bible is clear: God is jealous for his people.

Exodus 34:14: "*You must not bow down to another God, for Yahweh, his name is Jealous, is a jealous God.*"

His name is Jealous. That's who he is. He's jealous for us.

Exodus 20:5: "*You shall not bow down to them or serve them, for I, Yahweh your God, am a jealous God.*"

James 4:5: "*The Spirit who dwells in us is intensely jealous.*"

God is jealous when we turn to other things. When we pursue the world, when we bow down to idols (and idols can be anything we put before him—career, money, relationships, entertainment, comfort), when we violate our covenant with him—he is jealous.

And his jealousy is good. It's not petty or insecure. It's the righteous jealousy of a husband who knows his bride is meant for him alone and won't tolerate anything that threatens that relationship.

When we set ourselves as a seal on his heart, when we invite his jealousy, we're saying, "Lord, if I start to wander, if I start to be distracted, if I start to pursue other things—intervene. Do whatever it takes to bring me back. I give you permission to be jealous for me."

And he will.

If you're someone who has given your life to Jesus, who has said "Set me as a seal on your heart," and then you start dabbling in things that pull you away from him—don't be shocked when those things suddenly stop working. Don't be surprised when doors close, when plans fall apart, when what seemed like opportunities turn into dead ends.

That's not God being mean. That's God being jealous. That's him saying, "You've given me permission to keep you from wandering. You've asked me to set you as a seal. So I'm protecting this relationship."

I've seen this happen. I've watched as believers who started pursuing things that would pull them away from Jesus suddenly had those paths blocked. What looked like tragedy or disappointment was actually God's jealous love keeping them on track.

God can move powerfully when we've given him permission to be jealous for us.

The Cost of Intimacy

Here's what we need to understand: When God's power comes in fullness, when his presence manifests at high levels, the cost of sin increases dramatically.

Nadab and Abihu were freshly ordained priests. They offered unauthorized fire before the Lord, and they lost their lives instantly. It seems harsh until you realize that when God's presence is that strong, that manifest, that powerful—you can't trifle with it. You can't be casual about holiness.

Ananias and Sapphira lied to the Holy Spirit, and both of them dropped dead. People have lied to the Holy Spirit throughout church history without that consequence. But in that moment, in the early church when the Spirit was fully in control, the cost was immediate and severe.

It's not that God changed. It's that when his presence is fully manifest, when his power is operating at full strength, the consequences are immediate.

We're entering a season where God's power is coming to the Church at levels we haven't seen. Over the past years, the Lord has spoken to us using hurricane imagery. We are located in South Florida, so this speaks to us. He has told us repeatedly that there is a category five wave of his grace and glory coming. I'm convinced it is about to break on our shores. When it does, everything will change.

Living in the flesh, tolerating sin, being casual about holiness—all of that will become much more costly. Not because God is angry, but because his presence demands holiness. When the holy God is fully present, unholy things can't survive.

This is why the mature bride invites his jealousy. She's saying, "I want to be ready for the fullness of your presence. I want to be holy as you are holy. So set me as a seal. Be jealous for me. Don't let me wander. Keep me faithful even if it costs me everything else."

That's the level of commitment the mature bride has. That's what the wilderness has produced in her.

The Brothers Speak

"We have a young sister and she has no breasts. What should we do for our sister on the day when she is asked to marry? If she is a wall, we will build defenses of silver. And if she is a door, we will secure her with planks of cedar." (8:8-9)

Now we flash back to when the Shulammite was younger. Her brothers are discussing what to do with her when she reaches marriageable age. How do they keep her chaste for her future husband?

If she's a wall—if she's naturally chaste, not open to sweet-talkers—they'll adorn her with silver. They'll make her even more beautiful and help her stay pure.

If she's a door—if she's too open, too friendly with men—they'll cover her with cedar planks. They'll make her a wall whether she wants to be or not. They'll protect her honor even if she's not protecting it herself.

Brothers had this protective role in that culture. They watched over their sisters' reputations and virtue.

The Bride's Response

Now we come to the verse that came to me all night in a dream. This verse helped unlock the entire Song for me.

"I was a wall and my breasts became towers. Then in his eyes, I was as one who achieves peace." (8:10)

The Shulammite remembers her brothers' discussion, and she says, "I *was* a wall. I remained chaste. I preserved myself for my husband. And I matured—my breasts became towers."

Then the ultimate statement: "*Then in his eyes, I was as one who achieves peace.*"

In the eyes of her husband, she was one who achieved peace. She became peaceful. She took on the character of Solomon, whose name means peace.

Remember, she's called the Shulammite—the feminine form of Solomon. She's become like him. She's taken on his character. She reflects his nature.

Solomon is the Prince of Peace. Jesus is the ultimate Prince of Peace.

The mature bride reflects her husband's peace. This is the fruit of the Spirit being fully developed: Love, joy, peace, patience, kindness, goodness, faithfulness, gentleness, and self-control.

The bride has matured to the point where she reflects the peace of her Beloved. When people see her, they see his character. When they experience her presence, they experience his peace.

This is who the Church is called to be. Not anxious, not fearful, not panicking about what's happening in the world—but reflecting the supernatural peace of Jesus Christ.

In the days we're living in, this is key. The world is going to get more chaotic. Things are going to shake. People are going to be terrified.

The bride of Christ is going to stand in the middle of it all, leaning on her Beloved, reflecting his peace.

That's who this is. That's the answer to "Who is this coming up from the wilderness?"

This is the bride who has achieved peace. The one who reflects her husband's nature and character.

The Vineyard

"A vineyard in Baal Hamon belonged to Solomon. He gave the vineyard to those who care for vineyards. Each man was to bring a thousand silver coins for its fruit. My vineyard is my own to share. The thousand silver coins are for you, O Solomon, and the two hundred are for those who care for its fruit." (8:11-12)

This might seem like an odd tangent, but it's actually profound. Solomon has vineyards. He leases them out to tenant farmers who pay him for the privilege of working them and keeping some of the profit.

The bride says, "I have my own vineyard"—remember, the vineyard represents intimacy, ministry opportunity, the sphere of influence God has given you. "And I'm going to give you the full thousand silver coins. I'm giving you everything."

She's not keeping the profits for herself. She's not saying, "Well, I did the work, so I should get most of the benefit." She's saying, "It's all yours. Everything I produce is for you."

Then she adds, "Two hundred are for those who care for its fruit." Two hundred out of a thousand. That's twenty percent. That's double the normal tithe.

She's saying, "And I'm going to generously support those who help care for what you've given me."

This is the Proverbs 31 Church. The bride who doesn't just maintain her own relationship with Jesus, but who takes responsibility for his business. Who stewards well what he has given her. Who works to multiply the ministry opportunities. Who generously supports those who help in the work.

Paul picked up on this in 1 Timothy 5:17: "*The elders who manage well are worthy of double financial honor, especially those who labor in word and teaching.*"

Double honor, that is twenty percent instead of the normal ten percent for those who care for the fruit of the kingdom.

The mature bride understands. She gives everything to Jesus—the full thousand coins. She generously supports those who labor in ministry—the two hundred coins.

This is stewardship. This is taking responsibility. This is the bride acting as a partner in her husband's business, not just as a dependent.

Jesus wants a bride who will work with him, who will cooperate with him, who will take his assignments and multiply them, who will steward his kingdom faithfully.

That's what this passage is showing us.

The Final Exchange

"You women who sit in the gardens with companions listening attentively to your voice, make your voice heard for me." (8:13)

Solomon speaks. He's saying, "You're out there with your friends, and they are listening to you. I want to hear your voice too. Speak to me."

The husband longs to hear his bride's voice.

Jesus longs to hear our voices. He wants us to speak to him, to worship him, to pray to him. He wants our voice raised above the noise of the world.

We need to make our voice heard in the world—the voice of the Church speaking truth, proclaiming the gospel, standing for righteousness. But we also need to make our voice heard to Jesus—worship, prayer, intimate conversation with him.

He is saying, "Let me hear you."

The Bride's Final Words

"Escape, my lover, and let yourself be like a gazelle or a youthful stag among the stags on the mountain of spices." (8:14)

The Shulammite's final words are an invitation. She's used this imagery before—back at the beginning of their relationship, she pictured him bounding toward her like a gazelle, full of youthful energy and passion.

Now she invites him again: "Come to me with that same energy, that same passion, that same eagerness."

She's saying, "I want our relationship to stay fresh. I want the passion to remain. Come to me the way you did when we first fell in love."

That's where the Song ends. With the bride inviting the bridegroom to come.

The New Testament book of Revelation ends the same way. The Spirit and the bride say, "Come." And Jesus responds, "Yes, I am coming soon."

The mature bride doesn't just wait passively for Jesus' return. She actively invites him. "Come, Lord Jesus. Come in power. Come in glory. Come and finish what you started. Come and complete the work. Come and take your bride home."

That's the heart cry of the mature Church. She does not fear the end times. She is not trying to delay his coming. But she has eager anticipation: "Come quickly, Lord. We're ready. We've been refined in the wilderness. We've learned to always answer your knock. We've achieved your peace. We're reflecting your character. Come and get your bride."

The Revelation Complete

So who is this coming up from the wilderness leaning on her lover?

This is the mature bride.

The one who has been tested and refined.

The one who has learned never to refuse her Beloved when he knocks.

The one who is completely dependent on him, leaning on him for everything.

The one who reflects his peace even in chaos.

The one who takes responsibility for his business and stewards it faithfully.

The one who generously supports those who labor in his kingdom.

The one who makes her voice heard, both to him in worship and to the world in witness.

The one who eagerly invites him to come.

This is the bride Jesus is preparing. This is who the Church is called to be. This is the answer to the question.

This is why we needed to study the Song of Songs. Because we're entering the season when this bride needs to emerge. The world needs to see who the mature Church is. The chaos is coming, and people need to see believers who reflect the supernatural peace of Jesus Christ.

We need to be those who lean on him completely, who are sealed on his heart, who have invited his jealousy to keep us faithful, who give him everything, who can't wait for him to come.

That's the bride he is coming for.

That's who we're called to be.

The Song of Songs has shown us the way.

CONCLUSION

When Bobby Conner stood in our congregation and gave me the assignment to teach the Song of Songs, he said something I haven't forgotten: "The Church is about to have a whole makeover all across America."

A makeover.

Not a minor adjustment. Not a slight improvement. A complete transformation.

The bride is coming up out of the wilderness, and she's going to look different. She's going to act differently. She's going to have a level of maturity, authority, and power that we haven't seen in our generation.

We need to be ready for it.

What's Coming

I can hear it. I know that might sound strange, but I can hear the roar of what's coming. It's like standing on a beach and hearing the sound of a massive wave building out at sea. You can't see it yet, but you know it's there. You can feel it in your spirit.

It's a Category 5 wave of grace and glory. When it breaks on our shores, the Church will change.

The comfortable, casual Christianity we've known—where you can be a believer without much cost, where you can attend church without much commitment, where you can claim Jesus without looking much like him—that's going away.

When God's power comes in fullness, when his presence manifests at high levels, the cost of sin increases. The price of disobedience goes up. We're entering that kind of season.

The Necessity of Maturity

This is why the Song of Songs matters so much right now. This is why the Lord gave us this assignment in the Greatest of Songs. This is why the Lord had me study it, translate it, teach it.

Because we need to understand what a mature bride looks like. We need to know what God is working toward. We need to be prepared for the level of commitment and holiness that the coming wave will require.

The immature bride says, "Not tonight," when Jesus knocks. The mature bride leaps from bed, throws open the door, and says, "Yes, Lord, whatever you want, whenever you want it."

The immature bride is comfortable in religion but distant from relationship. The mature bride is completely dependent on Jesus, leaning on him for everything.

The immature bride pursues experiences without character development. The mature bride invites God's jealousy to keep her faithful, knowing the cost but willing to pay it.

The immature bride wants to keep some of her life for herself. The mature bride gives Jesus everything—all thousand silver coins—and holds nothing back.

We cannot remain immature and survive what's coming. We have to grow up. We have to mature. We have to become the bride Jesus deserves.

The Role of the Wilderness

Here's what we need to understand: The wilderness seasons we've been through—they were not punishment. They were preparation.

The times when God felt distant—he was teaching us to pursue him when we do not feel him.

The times when our prayers seemed to hit the ceiling—he was developing perseverance in us.

The times when we failed and faced consequences—he was showing us the importance of always answering his knock.

Every test, every trial, every wilderness season—it's all been preparation for what's coming.

The bride comes *up* from the wilderness. She is not defeated by it. She is not destroyed by it. She is refined by it, matured by it, transformed by it.

If you're in a wilderness right now, don't despair. Don't think God has abandoned you. He's preparing you. He's getting you ready for the Category 5 wave. He's making you into the bride who can handle the fullness of his presence and power.

Press through. Don't quit. Keep pursuing. Keep seeking. Keep leaning on him.

You're coming up from the wilderness. When you do, you'll be different. You'll be stronger. You'll be mature. You'll be leaning on Jesus.

Reflecting his Peace

The ultimate mark of the mature bride is that she "achieves peace" —she takes on the character of Solomon, the Prince of Peace. In our context, this means we reflect Jesus' peace even when the world is in chaos.

Jesus said, "Peace I leave with you. My peace I give to you. Not as the world gives do I give to you. Let not your hearts be troubled, neither let them be afraid."

The world's peace depends on circumstances. When things are good, there's peace. When things go bad, peace disappears.

Jesus' peace transcends circumstances. It's a supernatural peace that makes no sense to observers. It's the peace that comes from knowing who's in control, from trusting his promises, from leaning completely on him.

That's what the mature bride has. That's what the world is going to see in us. That's what's going to draw them to Jesus.

The Cost and the Glory

There's glory ahead—the glory of God manifest in his Church at levels we've never seen. The glory of miracles, signs, and wonders. The glory of multitudes coming to Christ. The glory of the bride finally looking like her Bridegroom.

But there's also cost. The cost of holiness when God's presence is fully manifest. The cost of obedience when the stakes are high. The cost of being set apart as his in a world that's hostile to him.

But here's the good news: If we're pursuing maturity now, if we're inviting God's jealousy to keep us faithful, if we're learning to always answer his knock, if we're leaning completely on him—we will be ready. We will be able to handle the fullness of his presence because we've been preparing for it. We will welcome his holiness because we've invited his jealousy. We will stand in his power—or rather, lean in his strength—because we've learned we can't do it ourselves.

The cost is real. But God's glory is worth it.

EPILOGUE

On a Sunday morning in early June of 2023, a prophet stood in our congregation and gave an assignment. At the time, I didn't fully understand. I knew it was from the Lord—the dream three weeks earlier had confirmed that—but I didn't know what we would discover in the Song of Songs.

Now, several years later, after translating every word from Hebrew, after studying many commentaries, after having a verse repeated to me all night in a dream until I understood its significance—now I know.

After I completed the assignment, I sent Bobby this summary: Who is this who comes? The mature bride who has spent time in the wilderness because she did not open the door when her Savior knocked. The mature bride who found out that the watchers of the world will bruise you and mock you when you have sent your king away. The mature bride who has learned to persevere and pursue, without being threatened by any other of her king's relationships and how he uses other believers. The mature bride who leans fully on him, recognizing that if she does not lean, she will fall. The mature bride who has taken on his nature of peace, and now reflects that peace back to him. The mature bride who now is busy with her husband's business, cultivating a vineyard for him, and supporting his workers.

The Song of Songs is about the mature bride. It's about who the Church is becoming. It's about the transformation that's happening right now in God's people as we prepare for the greatest outpouring of his Spirit the world has ever seen.

This isn't just ancient poetry. This isn't just a nice love story. This is prophetic. This is now. This is us.

God is preparing his bride. He's driving us to the wilderness so he can win us back with words of love. He's teaching us to always answer when he knocks. He's developing in us a supernatural peace that will astonish the world.

Not because we're perfect. But because we're mature.

The bride is coming up from the wilderness.

And she's beautiful.

SONG OF SONGS COMPLETE[7]

Chapter One

1Solomon's Song of Songs:

The Shulammite

2"Let him kiss me with the kisses from his mouth—for your
lovemaking[8] is sweeter than wine. 3Your lotions have an
aromatic fragrance, your name is oil poured from one vessel
to another, therefore the young women love you. 4Carry me
off after you, let us run!

"The king brought me to his bedroom."

The Daughters of Jerusalem

"Let us shout in exultation and delight in you; let us praise your lovemaking more than wine."

The Shulammite

"Rightly they love you."

5"I am dark but lovely, daughters of Jerusalem, like the tents of
Kedar, like the tent curtains of Solomon. 6Do not look at
me, for the sun has tanned me and my complexion is dark.
The sons of my mother have been angry with me. They

7 This is the complete "Unveiled" translation.

8 "Lovemaking" could also be translated "intimate love," "sexual intercourse," or "sexual intimacies." (See the use of this word inEzekiel 16:8 where the young woman is described as old enough for love—lovemaking.)

made me tend the vineyards, but my own vineyard I have
not tended.

7“Tell me, you who my soul loves, where do you graze your
flocks? Where do you give them rest at noon? For why
should I be like one who veils herself by the flocks of your
companions?”

Solomon

8“If you do not know by yourself, O loveliest of women, go out
following the hoof-prints of the flock, and graze your young
goats by the tents of the shepherds.

9“My intimate companion, I liken you to a mare for the
chariots of Pharaoh. 10Your cheeks are beautiful with
jewelry, your neck with strings of pearls.

11We will make jewelry of gold for you, studded with silver.”

The Shulammite

12“When the king was on his couch, my perfumed lotion
released its fragrance. 13My lover is a sachet of myrrh to me,
spending the night between my breasts. 14My lover is a
cluster of henna in the vineyards of Engedi.”

Solomon

15“Look how beautiful you are, my intimate companion, how
beautiful you are, your eyes are doves.”

The Shulammite

16“Look how handsome you are, my lover, and so pleasant.
Truly our bed is fresh and green. 17The timber-work of our
house is cedar; our rafters are juniper.”

Chapter Two

The Shulammite

1“I am the rose of Sharon, a lily of the valleys.”

Solomon

2“As a lily between the thorns, so my intimate companion is
among the daughters of Jerusalem.”

The Shulammite

3“As an apricot among the trees of the woodland, so my lover is
among the sons of Jerusalem. I delighted greatly and rested
in his shade, and his fruit was sweet to my taste. 4He
brought me to the vineyard, and his banner over me is love.

5“Refresh me with raisin cakes, spread out apricots for me, for I
am faint with love. 6His left hand is under my head, and his
right hand caresses me.

7“I earnestly urge you all, daughters of Jerusalem, by the
gazelles or by the deer of the field, do not arouse, do not stir
up sexual desire until love can take pleasure in it.

8“The voice of my lover! Look, he is coming, leaping over the
mountains, bounding over the hills. 9My lover is like a
gazelle or a youthful stag among the stags. Look, he is
standing behind our wall. He is watching through the
windows. He is looking through the lattice.

10“My lover responds to me and says,”

Solomon

“ ‘Arise, my intimate companion, my beautiful one, and come.
11For look, the winter has passed, the rain has finished and
gone by. 12The blossoms have appeared in the land, a time
for singing has arrived. The voice of the turtledove is heard
in our land. 13The fig tree has brought forth her figs, and the
blossoms of the vines have released their sweet smell. Arise,
come my intimate lover, my beautiful one, and come. 14My
dove in the clefts of the rock, in the shelter of the cliff, show
me your figure, let me hear your voice. For your voice is
sweet and your figure is lovely.’ ”

The Shulammite

15"Hold the foxes for us, the young foxes that are ruining the
vineyards, and our vineyards are in blossom. 16My lover is
mine and I am his; he grazes among the lilies 17until the day
begins and the shadows flee. Move around, my lover, be like
a gazelle, or a youthful stag upon the mountains by my
cleavage.[9]"

Chapter Three

The Shulammite

1"Upon my bed at night, I sought him whom my soul loves. I
sought him but did not find him. 2Let me arise now and
walk around in the city, in the streets and in the plazas. Let
me seek the one my soul loves. I sought him but did not
find him. 3Those who keep watch doing their rounds in the
city found me. I asked, 'Have you seen the one whom my
soul loves?'

4"A moment after I passed by them, I found the one whom my
soul loves. I held him and did not stop until I had brought
him to the house of my mother, and to the room of the one
who conceived me.

5"I earnestly urge you all, daughters of Jerusalem, by the
gazelles or by the deer of the field, do not arouse, do not stir
up sexual desire until love can take pleasure in it."

The Daughters of Jerusalem

6"What is this coming up from the wilderness like columns of
smoke perfumed with myrrh and frankincense, with all the
scented spices of the traders? 7Look, it is the sedan chair of
Solomon, sixty mighty men surround it of the mighty men
of Israel. 8All of them are holding a sword, all are skilled in

---

9 Because of the overtly sexual nature of this passage, and the fact that grazing among the lilies refers to lovemaking, valley is best translated "cleavage" (so also NASB in footnote)

battle, each man with his sword on his thigh against the dread of the nights.

9“King Solomon has made for himself a sedan chair, from the
trees of Lebanon. 10He made its posts of silver, its seat-back
of gold, its seat of purple; its interior is inlaid with love by
the daughters of Jerusalem. 11Go out, daughters of Zion,
and look upon King Solomon with the nuptial crown with
which his mother crowned him on the day of his wedding,
on the day of his heart’s elation.”

Chapter Four

Solomon

1“Know that you are beautiful, my intimate companion, know
that you are beautiful! Your eyes are doves behind your veil,
your hair is like a flock of goats that leap down from Mount
Gilead. 2Your teeth are like a flock of sheep shorn clean, that
have come up from their washing; all of them bearing twins,
and there is not one among them bereaved of her young.
3Your lips are like a scarlet thread, and your voice is lovely.
Like halves of a pomegranate are your cheeks behind your
veil. 4Your throat is like the tower of David, built with
courses of stones; a thousand shields are hung upon it, all
the quivers of the mighty men. 5Your two breasts are like
two fawns, twins of a gazelle that grazed among the lilies.

6“Until the day begins, and the shadows flee, I will myself go to
the mountain of myrrh and to the hill of frankincense.

7“Every part of you is beautiful, my intimate companion, and
there is no blemish in you. 8Come with me from Lebanon,
my bride, come with me from Lebanon! Travel with me
from the mountaintop of Amana, from the mountaintop of
Senir, from the mountaintop of Herman, from the dwelling
places of lions and the hill-country of leopards.

9“You have seduced me, my sister, my bride, you have seduced
me with one glance from your eyes, with one pearl of your
necklace. 10How attractive are your sexual intimacies, my
sister, my bride! How pleasing are your sexual moves, more
than wine; and the fragrance of your lotions is more pleasing
than all the spices. 11Your lips drip flowing honey, my bride;
honey and milk are under your tongue, and the fragrance of
your clothing is like the fragrance of Lebanon.”

12“You are a garden that is locked, my sister, my bride, a
fountain that is locked, a spring that is sealed. 13Your
branches are a forest of pomegranates with choice fruit,
henna, and nard plants, 14nard and saffron, cane and
cinnamon, with all the trees of frankincense, myrrh, and
aloes, including the best spices. 15You are spring for the
gardens, a well of living waters, and streams flowing from
Lebanon.”

The Shulammite

16“Awaken, O north wind; and come, O south wind. Make the scent of my garden waft out. Let its perfume be poured out. May my lover come to his garden and eat its choice fruits.”

Chapter Five

Solomon

1“I have come to my garden, my sister, my bride; I have plucked my myrrh with my spice. I have eaten my honeycomb with my honey; I have drunk my wine with my milk.”

Daughters of Jerusalem

“Eat, lovers! Drink and be drunk on sexual intimacies.”

The Shulammite

2“I was asleep, but my heart was awake. A sound, my lover is knocking!”

Solomon

“Open to me, my sister, my intimate companion, my dove, my
perfect one; for my head is covered with dew, my strands of
hair with the moisture of the night.”

The Shulammite

3“I have taken off my gown, how can I possibly put it on? I
have washed my feet, how can I soil them?

4“My lover put his hand to the opening, and my intimate parts
were aroused for him. 5I got ready to open for my lover. My
hand dripped with myrrh, and my fingers with flowing
myrrh on the handles of the lock. 6I opened for my lover,
but my lover had turned away, he had gone his way. My soul
went out as he turned his back. I tried to search for him but
did not find him. I called him, but he did not answer.

7“Those who keep watch doing their rounds in the city found
me. They struck and bruised me. They took my veil away
from me, the ones who watch the walls.

8“I earnestly urge you all, daughters of Jerusalem, if you find my
lover, this is what you should say to him: I am faint with
love.”

The Daughters of Jerusalem

9“What is your lover more than another lover, O loveliest of
women? What is your lover more than another lover that
you so earnestly entreat us?”

The Shulammite

10“My lover is radiant and red, prominent among ten thousand.
11His head is like gold that is refined; his strands of hair are
waving palm branches, black as a raven. 12His eyes are like
doves upon streams of waters, bathed in milk, dwelling
beside a pool. 13His cheeks are like garden beds of spice,
terraces of fragrant spice; his lips are lilies dripping with

flowing myrrh. 14His hands are rods of gold set with topaz; his genitals are polished ivory trimmed with sapphires. 15His thighs are columns of alabaster established on bases of refined gold; his physique is like Lebanon, chosen like the cedars. 16His mouth is sweet, and he is entirely desirable. This is my lover, this is my companion, O daughters of Jerusalem."

Chapter Six

The Daughters of Jerusalem

1"Where has your lover gone, O loveliest of women? Where has your lover turned, so that we might seek him with you?"

The Shulammite

2"My lover has gone to his garden, to the garden beds of spice, to graze in the gardens and to gather lilies. 3I am my lover's, and my lover is mine. He grazes among the lilies."

Solomon

4"You are beautiful as Tirzah, my intimate companion, as lovely as Jerusalem, awe-inspiring as troops arrayed by their divisions. 5Let your eyes wander from me, for they overpower me; your hair is like a flock of goats that have leaped down from Gilead. 6Your teeth are like a flock of ewes that have come down from their washing, all of them bearing twins, and there is not one among them bereaved of her young. 7Like halves of a pomegranate are your cheeks behind your veil.

8"There are sixty queens, and eighty concubines, and virgins too numerous to count; 9but my dove, my perfect one is first, she is her mother's first daughter; she is pure to the one who bore her. The daughters of Jerusalem saw her and pronounced her blessed, the queens and concubines saw her, and they praised her."

Daughters of Jerusalem, Queens, and Concubines

10“Who is this woman that looks out like the dawn, lovely as
the full moon, pure as the sun, as awe-inspiring as troops
arrayed by their divisions.”

The Shulammite

11“I went down into the orchard among the nut trees to look at
the greenness of the valley, to see if the vine has flourished
and the pomegranates had blossomed. 12Before I knew it,
my soul directed me to the chariots of my noble people.”

The Charioteers

13“Move back, move back, O Shulammite; move back, move
back and let us look upon you.”

The Daughters of Jerusalem

“Why would you look upon the Shulammite, as at the Dance Of The Two Armies?”

Chapter Seven

Solomon

1“How attractive are your feet, visible in sandals, O noble's
daughter! The curves of your hips are like jewelry, the work
of a craftsman's hand. 2Your navel is a round drinking cup, it
does not lack spiced wine. Your mons pubis[10] is a mound of
wheat encircled by lilies. 3Your two breasts are like two
fawns, twins of a gazelle. 4Your neck is like a tower of ivory.
Your eyes are pools in Heshbon by the gates of Bath-
Rabbim. Your nose is like the tower of Lebanon facing
Damascus. 5Your head is upon you like Carmel, and the hair
of your head is like purple thread. The king is captured by
your locks of hair.

10 Alternately, “pubic mound,” or “vulva.”

6“How attractive and how delightful you are, O love, with all
your pleasures. 7Your stature is like a date palm tree, and
your breasts are its clusters.

8“I said, ‘I will climb the date palm. I will grasp the dates.’ Now
may your breasts be like clusters of the vine, and the breath
of your nostrils like apricots. 9And may your mouth be like
the best wine.”

The Shulammite

10“I am my lover's, and his sexual desire is focused on me.
11Come, my lover, let us go into the fields; let us spend the
night in the villages. 12Let us get up early and go to the
vineyards; let us see if the vine has budded, whether the
blossom has opened, whether the pomegranates are
flourishing. There I will make love with you. 13The
mandrakes have released their fragrance; and over our doors
are all precious gifts, new and old. I have kept them stored
away for you, my lover.”

Chapter Eight

The Shulammite

1“What if you were designated as a brother to me, an infant at
the breasts of my mother? I would find you outside and I
would kiss you, and they would not feel contempt for me. 2I
would lead you, I would bring you to the house of my
mother who taught me. I would give you spiced wine to
drink from the sweet juice of my pomegranates.

3"His left hand is under my head, and his right hand caresses
me.

4“I earnestly urge you all, daughters of Jerusalem, do not arouse,
do not stir up sexual desire until love can take pleasure in it.”

The Daughters of Jerusalem

5"Who is this coming up from the wilderness leaning against her lover?"

The Shulammite

"Under the apricot tree I aroused you; there your mother was pregnant with you, there she went into labor and gave birth to you.

6"Set me as a seal upon your heart, as a seal upon your arm, for sexual desire is as powerful as death, jealous passion is severe as Sheol. Its flames are flames of fire, the lightning of
Yahweh.[11] 7Many waters are not able to extinguish love's sexual desire, nor rivers flood it; if a man gave all the wealth of his house for it, they would surely despise him."

Brothers of the Shulammite

8"We have a young sister, and she has no breasts. What should we do for our sister on the day when she is asked to marry?
9If she is a wall, we will build defenses of silver; and if she is a door, we will secure her with planks of cedar."

The Shulammite

10"I was a wall, and my breasts became towers; then, in his eyes, I was as one who achieves peace.

11"A vineyard in Baal-Hamon belonged to Solomon; he gave the vineyard to those who care for vineyards. Each man was to bring a thousand silver coins for its fruit.

12"My vineyard is my own to share. The thousand silver coins are for you, O Solomon, and two hundred are for those who care for its fruit."

---

11 God's personal name (called the Tetragrammaton), Yahweh, is most often written as LORD in modern translations. It is also translated by some as Jehovah.

Solomon

13"You women who sit in the gardens, your husbands are listening attentively for your voice. Make your voices heard for me."

The Shulammite

14"Escape, my lover, and let yourself be like a gazelle or a youthful stag among the stags on the mountain of spices."

ABOUT THE AUTHOR

Randal Cutter is the founding pastor of New Dawn Community Church in Coral Springs, Florida.

Randal is a dynamic teacher of God's truth. He has studied Greek and Hebrew extensively and informs his teaching with appropriate references. He has a theologian's perspective on biblical truth and a pastor's heart for applying living truth.

In addition to his pastoral duties, he is also an Elder for the MorningStar Fellowship of Ministries, an organization that provides relational covering for ministries around the world. Randal has been an ordained member of the Fellowship of Ministries since its inception in 1995. In the past, he has also been an adjunct professor of the Greek language for MorningStar University's College of Theology. He has travelled extensively to teach the Word and impart clarity, prophetic vision, and insight.

His first book, *Whatever You Bind on Earth: Authority Over Hurricanes*, has transformed the way that many in the body perceive authority in prayer. His second book, *Created to Prosper*, has helped Christians around the world learn how to step into God's supernatural economy. He has also published a translation of the New Testament titled, *The New Charismatic Bible: The New Testament*. All his books and translations are available on Amazon and at other Christian bookstores.

Randal has been married to Dawn since 1980. They have three adult children, Alyssa, Linea, and Joshua, and two grandchildren.

www.ingramcontent.com/pod-product-compliance
Lightning Source LLC
LaVergne TN
LVHW010950110826
845149LV00015B/3286